MEN-AT-ARMS SERIES

EDITOR: MARTIN WINDROW

Napoleon's German Allies (5):

Hessen-Darmstadt & Hessen-Kassel

Text by OTTO VON PIVKA

Colour plates by BRYAN FOSTEN

OSPREY PUBLISHING LONDON

Published in 1982 by
Osprey Publishing Ltd
Member company of the George Philip Group
12–14 Long Acre, London WC2E 9LP

ISBN 0 85045 431 X

Filmset in Great Britain
Printed in Hong Kong

Acknowledgements

My sincere thanks are due to the following organisations and individuals who were so helpful in the provision of information for this book:

The directors and staff of the Museum Preussische Kulturbesitz, Berlin (Frau Doktor Gretel Wagner); Ministry of Defence Library, Whitehall (Mr Andrews, Mr Potts, Miss Glover); Gesamthochschul-Bibliothek Kassel; the Hessisches Staatsarchive Kassel, Marburg and Darmstadt; the Wehrhistorisches-und Jagdmuseum, Schloss Friedrichstein, Bad Wildungen; Herr Gross-Löscher; Herr Alfred Umhey and Herr Markus Gärtner of the Klio Arbeitsgruppe Waterloo; finally, to Sue Cook, and to my wife.

The Hessian Lands

The process of dividing inherited lands between all surviving male beneficiaries, which steadily reduced Germany to a trivial conglomeration of petty principalities over a period of centuries, was responsible for the splitting of Hessen-Kassel and Hessen-Darmstadt in 1567. The subsequent story of acquisitions and losses over 250 years is too complex to describe here. Suffice it that both states fought against France in the Revolutionary Wars; Darmstadt, on her own account as part of the Holy Roman Empire, and Kassel as a result of the latest in a series of subsidy deals by which she provided troops for the English crown. In 1795 Hessen-Kassel made peace with France at Basle. Hessen-Darmstadt, under the Landgraf Ludwig X, made peace in 1801 at Luneville.

In 1803 both states were enlarged by a sharing-out of previously Imperial free towns and church-states to compensate them for lands lost to France. In addition, Landgraf Wilhelm of Hessen-Kassel secured the coveted title of 'Kurfürst' (Prince Elector of the Holy Roman Empire).

In 1806 Hessen-Darmstadt was to grow even larger under the patronage of Napoleon. Joining the Rheinbund in that year, she received all remaining Imperial possessions within her borders, and Landgraf Ludwig became Grossherzog Ludwig when his state was elevated to a Grand Duchy by Napoleon.

Hessen-Kassel's fate was very different. Kurfürst Wilhelm I enraged Napoleon by partially mobilising his army when France attacked Prussia in October 1806; and the following month the French dictator took his revenge by dissolving Hessen-Kassel and incorporating it into his brother Jerome's new Kingdom of Westfalia (see MAA 43, *Napoleon's German Allies (1): Berg and Westfalia)*. In November 1813 Wilhelm returned from exile, resumed the now-empty title of Kurfürst, and set about trying to put the political, administrative, social and sartorial clock back to 1806.

Centrepiece of a Hessen-Kassel officer's gorget, *c.*1788; gold supporters and frame, coloured enamel centre, originally mounted on a silver gorget. (Schloss Friedrichstein Museum)

In 1814 the Congress of Vienna made further changes to the borders of Hessen-Darmstadt, and accordingly Ludwig's title became 'Grossherzog von Hessen und bei Rhein'.

Hessen-Darmstadt: Organisation and Uniforms, 1792

Establishment of Infantry Regiments, 1792

Each regiment had two battalions each of four companies of two platoons. A grenadier or musketeer company consisted of: 1 captain, 2 lieutenants, 1 sergeant major, 2 sergeants, 1 corporal, 3 lance corporals, 1 fifer, 2 drummers

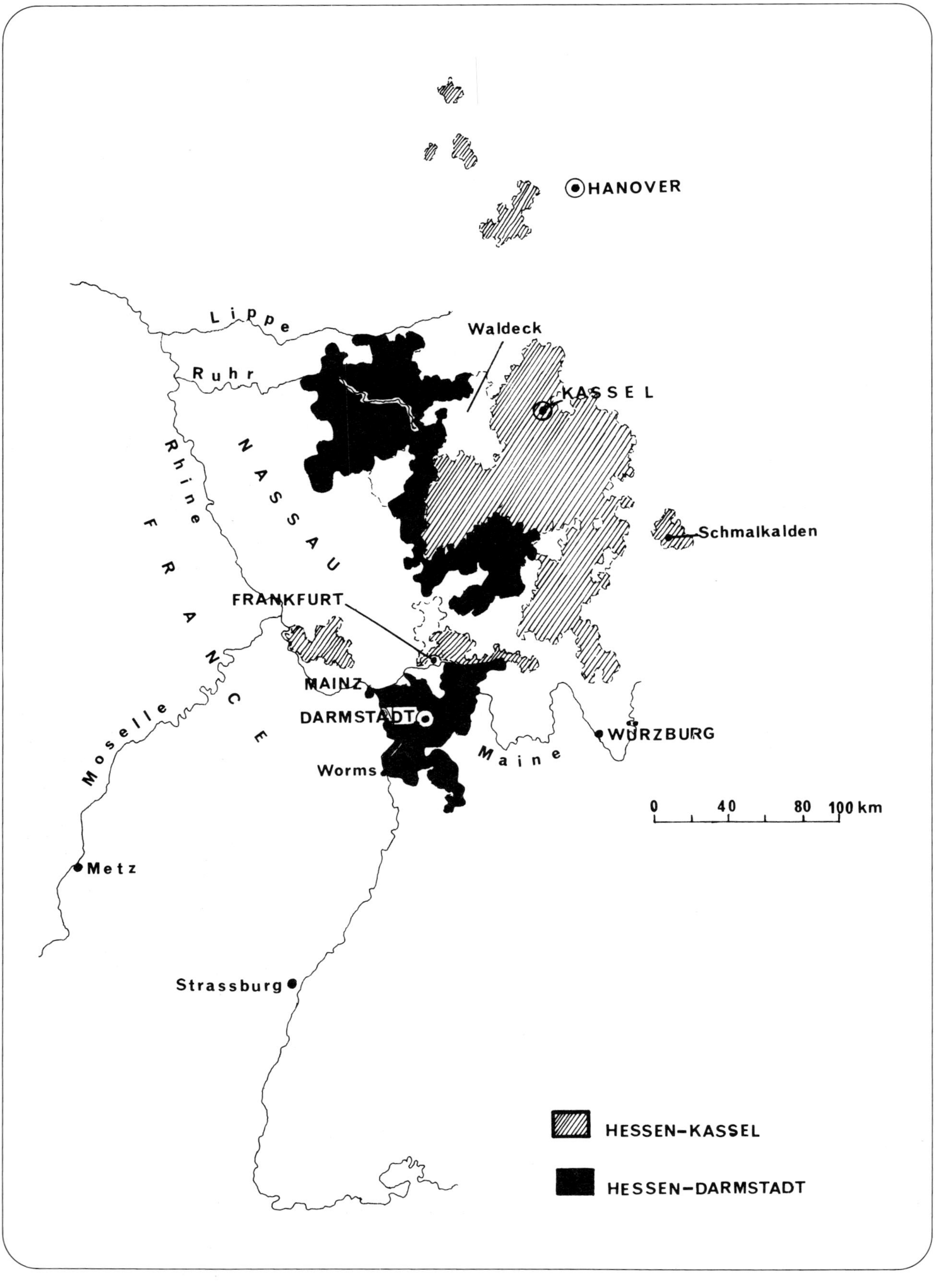
HANOVER
Lippe
Ruhr
Waldeck
KASSEL
Rhine
NASSAU
FRANCE
Schmalkalden
FRANKFURT
MAINZ
DARMSTADT
Worms
WÜRZBURG
Maine
Moselle
0
40
80
100 km
Metz
Strassburg
HESSEN-KASSEL
HESSEN-DARMSTADT

Crests of Hessen-Kassel:
Top, Landgrafschaft, 1794: Central shield, red-and-white striped Hessian lion, with golden crown and sword, on blue ground. Peripheral shields, clockwise from 1 o'clock: six-point silver star on black over a golden field – County of Ziegenhain; two gold rampant leopards on red field – County of Diez; silver-over-red shield surrounded by three silver nails and three silver parts of a nettle leaf – County of Schaumburg; quartered, red-and-gold heraldic ordinaries (Principality of Hanau), red-and-gold horizontal bars (County of Reineck), the central shield gold over red (Herrschaft Münzenberg); two eight-point silver stars on a black field over a gold field – County of Nidda; rampant red lion with blue crown, on red ground – County of Katzenelnbogen; red cross of Lorraine on white ground – Archbishopric of Lorraine and Principality of Hersfeld. The Order of the Garter surrounds the crest.

Bottom, Electorate, 1806: The fields, though re-arranged, basically as 1794 but with addition of two: at 1 o'clock, a gold upright cross on blue (Principality of Fritzlar, 1803); and a silver central shield – significance unknown.

and 90 privates. A battalion thus had 1 major (commander), 3 captains, 1 'staff-captain' (who commanded the major's company), 8 lieutenants, 1 adjutant, 28 NCOs, 12 fifers and drummers and 360 privates. The regimental commander (usually a lieutenant-colonel) always served with the 1st (or Leib) Battalion, and the regimental staff included the quartermaster, padre, auditor, surgeon, armourer, musket carpenter, provost, regimental and battalion drum majors. Company surgeons were ranked as NCOs and were supernumerary to the figures quoted above.

Drill and Tactics

Companies formed in three ranks; in the 1st Bn. the regimental commander's company (Leib-Kompagnie) formed on the right of the line, the battalion commander's company on the left. Apart from the Leib-Kompagnie all companies were known by the names of their commanders and were arranged in line in accordance with the relative seniority of that officer within the battalion. When companies changed commanders they also changed position in line of battle if an alteration in relative seniority had taken place. In the 1st Bn. the senior captain's company took place next to the Leib-Kompagnie, the junior captain's being third in line. In the 2nd Bn. the battalion commander's company was on the right wing, the senior captain's on the left wing, the others in the centre.

In the spring recruits were trained for four weeks and then posted to their companies. During the summer each company was maintained at full strength for the annual training period which started with drill at company level (six weeks), and progressed through battalion and regimental (sometimes to brigade) exercises, culminating in a manoeuvre under the eyes of the sovereign. For the rest of the year most of the men were sent home (after having handed in their equipment and weapons – cavalry troopers often took their horses with them) to live as best they could without pay until the annual training cycle began again. Company strength was thus reduced to the officers, NCOs and about 30 privates. Garrison life in autumn, winter and spring was taken up with guard duty and a short daily parade at guard-changing.

Arms drill was simplified in comparison to earlier periods. Loading, in 13 separate movements, was usually carried out from the 'order arms' position, but could be initiated from the 'shoulder arms' as well. When firing, the front rank knelt. Fire was given by the platoon of the company, or the battalion of the regiment, the other half of the formation reserving its fire in each case to cover those men who had fired and were committed to the long and vulnerable re-

Two tunics, apparently of troopers of the Hessen-Kassel Garde du Corps, *c.*1798 – white, crimson facings, silver lace and buttons. Note shoulder strap button on collar itself, and placing of strap to rear of shoulder. In the foreground is the Pallasch sword carried by this regiment: brass hilt, 'WL' cypher on basket, black and gold-wire grip. (Schloss Friedrichstein Museum)

loading process. Another tactice used was the 'Heckenfeuer', in which an officer walked down the rear rank from the right of the line giving fire orders progressively to groups of three files (i.e. nine men). Live musketry practice was supposed to take place during three weeks per year, but economy (or the corruption of company commanders, who paid for the ammunition) often reduced this.

The rate of marching was 75 paces per minute; in 1793 a 'Doublierschritt' or double-march was introduced for changing position on the battlefield. In 1808 the custom of re-arranging the companies in the line for each change of commander was abolished; and although the three-rank line was retained as the normal formation, a two-rank line was introduced and practised. Light infantry were drilled like line infantry, but also in extended order skirmishing tactics and field outpost duty.

Each battalion had two 3-pdr. cannon, their detachments commanded by an artillery officer; in action these were normally posted on each flank.

Re-organisation of May/November 1803, 1806

A Feld-Brigade and a Garnison-Brigade were raised in each of the three main provinces (Starkenburg, Oberhessen and Westfalen), the latter soon being retitled Reservebrigaden. These were a type of Landwehr, composed of the cadres only of two battalions each, and bore the name of the province. The field brigades were named and composed as follows:

Starkenburg – 'Leib-Brigade'; Leib-Regiment and Füsilier-Bataillon (formerly Leichtes-Infanterie-Regiment, see below); main garrison at Darmstadt.

Oberhessen – 'Brigade Landgraf'; Regiment Landgraf and new Füsilier-Bataillon (formerly 2nd Leib-Grenadier-Bataillon); two bns. at Giessen, one at Alsfeld.

Westfalen – 'Brigade Erbprinz'; Regiment Erbprinz and Füsilier-Bataillon Erbprinz; garrisons at Brilon, Werl and Arnsberg.

On 18 August 1806 titles were changed when Landgraf Ludwig X became Grossherzog Ludwig I. The Leib-Bde. became the Leib-Garde-Bde., with the Leib-Garde-Regt. and the Garde-Füsilier-Bn.; the Brigade Landgraf became the Leib-Bde., with the Leib-Regt. and the 1st Leib-Füsilier-Bn.; and the Brigade Erbprinz became the Brigade Gross- und Erbprinz, with the Regt. Gross- und Erbprinz and the 2nd Leib-Füsilier-Bn. (At the same time the Chevaulegers-Regt. became the Garde-Chevaulegers-Regt. – see under 'Cavalry', below.)

In 1803 the infantry company establishment was 1 captain or staff-captain, 2 lieutenants, 1 sergeant major, 2 sergeants, 4 corporals, 3 drummers and fifers, 7 sharpshooters and 83 privates: 103 in all. The staff of a four-company battalion was 1 major or lieutenant-colonel, 1 subaltern, 1 senior surgeon, 1 clerk, 2 junior surgeons, 1 drum major, 8 musicians, and one provost. The battalion total was thus 428 all ranks.

The totals for a three-battalion brigade were:

1 colonel, 1 lieutenant-colonel, 2 majors, 8 captains, 4 staff-captains, 12 first lieutenants, 16 second lieutenants (incl. 1 brigade and 3 battalion adjutants), 1 staff quartermaster, 1 staff auditor, 1 staff surgeon, 1 priest, 2 senior surgeons, 12 sergeant majors, 24 sergeants, 48 corporals, 1 brigade clerk, 3 battalion clerks, 6 junior surgeons, 3 drum majors, 24 musicians, 36 drummers and fifers, 3 provosts, 84 sharpshooters, and 996 privates: in all, 1,291 all ranks.

Uniforms, 1792

All matters of finance and clothing lay in the hands of the company commanders – the 'chefs', or, essentially, owners of their companies. Uniforms, discipline, tactics and organisation were also closely modelled on the Prussian example. Hair was powdered, curled, and worn in a pigtail extending to the small of the back; moustaches were not worn except as specifically noted below. Officers' sashes and sword knots were silver and red. Black cockades were worn on black Prussian-style bicorn hats, with white and red plumes for officers and NCOs. The specifics of the various arms and ranks are listed below.

N.B. For reasons of space the following abbreviations have been adopted for the uniform sections throughout this book:

Offs. = Officers
ORs = Other ranks
HL = Hat lace (edging)
CLR = Collar
C = Cuffs
CF = Cuff flaps
HPF = Hip pocket flap
L = lapels
TB = turn-backs
B = breeches
BTN = buttons
W = waistcoat
F = facings

Major-Generals, Town Commandants Wide, scalloped silver HL & White cut-feather edging; silver star below cockade, silver cords, tassels red-within-silver. Dark blue coat and CF; red C, L, CLR; white TB; silver BTN. White W, B; high cuffed boots; sword.

Infantry Flügel-Adjutants (ADCs) Plain bicorn with star, cockade, cords as above. Sky blue coats and CF; red C, L, CLR; silver right-hand aiguillette fastened to third L BTN; silver laced buttonhole – seven on each L, two under each L, three on each CF, two on each HPF, two in small of back. White W, B; boots, sword, as above.

Cavalry General-Adjutants (ADCs) As infantry except: white plume, red base. The CLR bore sky blue patches with a horizontal silver lace in centre. No CF; on each C a silver lace chevron, point down, and two more above the C. Three more chevrons extended down the tails, replacing HPFs.

Infantry officers 'à la suite de l'Armée' (on general staff) As major-generals, but hat lacked silver HL and cut-feather trim. *Cavalry officers 'à la suite de l'Armée'* Hat as cavalry ADC. White coat and CF; red CLR, L, C, TB; silver BTN, right-hand aiguillette; buff W, B; high, cuffed boots. Black waist belt over W, silver/rectangular plate, steel-hilted sabre in black sheath, steel fittings.

Grenadier cap of an NCO, unidentified Hessen-Kassel regiment, 1785–1806. The front plate is silver, the cloth headpiece or backing white with silver lace trim, the headband yellow edged with silver, and the top tassel red and white. (Schloss Friedrichstein Museum)

Grenadier cap plates of various unidentified Hessen-Kassel regiments, 1785–1806: left and centre are in white metal, right in brass, with a 'WL' cypher in the centre field. (Schloss Friedrichstein Museum)

Line Infantry – General Notes

Officers' parade and duty bicorns had wide, scalloped lace edging and star brooches in 'button colour' (except where otherwise specified), black cockades, and silver-and-red cords and tassels. Boots were knee-high, those of grenadier officers having knee cuffs; waistcoats and breeches were white; coats dark blue; and gauntlets buff. They carried brown canes with gilt knobs and silver tassels.

Corporals had silver lace at the top and front of the cuffs, sergeants and sergeant majors laced cuffs and collars. All NCOs had button-colour hat edging, and white pompons with red centres; red and white sabre knots; and carried rifles instead of muskets. They had brown canes with brass knobs and red and white tassels. On the black cartridge pouch flap they wore a round brass plate bearing the Hessian lion.

Privates' hats had white edging; they bore a regimental button under a pompon in company colours, and white cords with red-within-white tassels. Their Prussian infantry sabres had brown sheaths, and white fist straps with a company-coloured tassel. These colours were: *1st Bn.* 1st (or Leib-) Kompagnie, white; 2nd, black; 3rd, blue; 4th, red. *2nd Bn.* 5th, yellow; 6th, black-over-white; 7th, blue-over-white; 8th, red-over-white. Belts, waistcoats and breeches were white, the long gaiters black with brass buttons. Coats were dark blue with red turn-backs; an oblong of regimental facing cloth backed the button fastening these. Ten sharpshooters per company carried rifles. Drummers, and hornists of light infantry, were distinguished by swallows' nests in facing colour with a bottom band of white lace. Drums were brass with red and white hoops.

Individual regimental title changes and uniform distinctions were as follows:

Leib-Regiment

1 June 1803, Leib-Brigade, with 2nd Füsilier-Bataillon; 18 August 1806, Leib-Garde-Brigade, two bns. Leib-Garde-Regt. and Garde-Füsilier-Bn.; 22 February 1812, Leib-Garde-Regt. of two bns.; 1918, Inf.-Regt. Nr. 115.

Red F, silver BTN. Buttonholes laced, silver for offs., white for ORs, with end opposite button pointed.

Regiment Landgraf

1 June 1803, Brigade Landgraf; 18 August 1806, Leib-Brigade, two bns. Regt. Landgraf and Leib-Füsilier-Bn.; 22 February 1812, Leib-Regt. of two bns.; 1918, Nr. 117.

White F, gold BTN; 1803, light blue F, silver BTN. Buttonholes laced, tasselled, gold for offs., white for ORs except on L which bore BTN only.

Regiment Erbprinz

A garrison regiment in 1792; 8 December 1794, Feld-Bataillon Erbprinz raised (1st Bn. of regt.): 1 June 1803, Brigade Erbprinz, two line bns. (2nd Bn. being former Inf.-Regt. von Kleist taken over from disbanded Electorate of Köln) and 1st Füsilier-Bn. (ex-1st Leib-Grenadier-Bn.); 18 August 1806, Brigade Gross- und Erbprinz, two line bns., 1st Füsilier-Bn. being renamed 2nd Leib-Füsilier-Bn.; 22 August 1808, Regt. Gross- und Erbprinz, two bns. each of one grenadier, one voltigeur and four fusilier companies. Destroyed in Spain; re-raised from returned prisoners and new recruits 7 May 1814, two bns. each of four companies; 1918, Nr. 118.

Pink F (1803, yellow), silver BTN. Silver laced buttonholes for offs., white for ORs.

1st Leib-Grenadier-Bataillon

26 November 1799, 1st Füsilier-Bn.; 1 June 1803, attached as Füsilier-Bn. to Brigade Erbprinz; 18 August 1806, 2nd Leib-Füsilier-Bn.; 23 August

1808, amalgamated with line bns. into Regt. Gross- und Erbprinz; 1918, Nr. 118.

Crimson F (yellow, June 1803), silver BTN. Silver laced buttonholes for offs., with tassels. ORs wore white laced buttonholes; and silver flaming grenade badge on musketeers' bicorns in place of button, inclined left.

2nd Leib-Grenadier-Bataillon

Disbanded 1803, most personnel to new Füsilier-Bn., see below.

Orange F, gold BTN. Offs. had gold buttonhole lacing. ORs had white buttonhole lace, and brass flaming grenade, inclined left, replaced hat button.

Depot Battalion

No offs. HL; dull yellow F, unlaced buttonholes.

Land-Regiment

A type of home guard. No offs. HL; light blue F, silver BTN. Only ORs buttonhole lace, and this only under each L (two), on C (three), and on HPF (two).

Marxburg Fortress Garrison

Yellow F, dark blue L, silver BTN. Offs. wore plain bicorn, silver right-hand aiguillette. No buttonhole lace.

Infantry Surgeons

Plain bicorn with silver loop and button, black cockade. Green coat, CLR, C, CF, L; red TB; silver BTN; white W, B; black gaiters, sword.

Medical Attendant

Inf. ORs' bicorn, no edging. Dark blue coat, CLR, C, CF, L; red TB. Dark blue W, B; silver BTN; black gaiters, inf. sabre.

Provost

Bicorn with green edging and pompon. Grey coat, CF; green CLR, C, L, TB, aiguillette; silver BTN; green W, B; black gaiters, inf. sabre.

Light Infantry – General Notes

Officers' bicorns had narrow button-colour edging, ORs' white edging. Officers wore short, light boots, and carried curved sabres. Officers wore epaulettes in button-colour, ORs shoulder straps in facing colour. Coats were in a light green; all other details followed line infantry practice, except where specified below.

Leichtes Infanterie-Bataillon

26 November 1799, 2nd Füsilier-Bn.; 1 June 1803,

Model of Hessen-Kassel howitzer, *c*.1785. (Schloss Friedrichstein Museum)

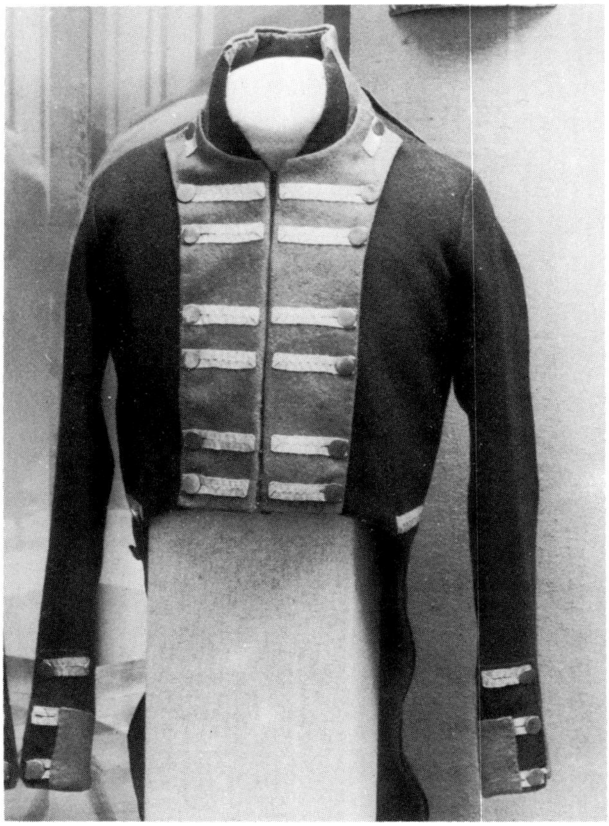

Tunic of a private, Hessen-Darmstadt Leib-Regiment, *c*.1795. Dark blue coat faced red, white lace, silver buttons. Note the unusual collar, indicating Hessen-Darmstadt; the rear placing of the shoulder strap and the lace and buttons set below the lapels are also visible. The Schloss Friedrichstein Museum authorities were in fact unable to identify this Hessen-Darmstadt uniform, which found its way to them in about 1900 from the Kassel theatre, where many items now in the museum had been used for costume pieces! (Schloss Friedrichstein Museum)

attached to Leib-Brigade as 1st Leib-Füsilier-Bn.; 18 August 1806, Garde-Füsilier-Bn.; April 1812, combined with 1st Leib-Füsilier-Bn. as 'Provisorisches Leichtes Infanterie-Regiment'; 17 June 1813, provisional title confirmed as Garde-Füsilier-Regt.; 1918, Inf.-Regt. Kaiser Wilhelm (2 Grossherzoglich Hessiches) Nr. 116.

1792, black F, gold BTN; 1799, silver BTN; June 1803, field poppy red F; 1813, silver chin-scales added to shako.

Füsilier-Bataillon

Raised 1803 from disbanded 2nd Leib-Grenadier-Bn., see above, and attached to Brigade Landgraf, later the Leib-Brigade, thus from 18 August 1806 this unit became 1st Leib-Füsilier-Bn.; April 1812, combined with Garde-Fusilier-Bn. in 'Provisorische Leichte Inf.-Regt', see above.

1803, light green coat, light blue F, silver BTN. Offs. had short white gloves, ORs wore line inf. hats, NCOs with silver HL. Silver or white lace, according to rank, on L, CF, HPF, and other usual points of coat.

Jäger Corps

Disbanded 'shortly after 1796' (Knötel). All ranks, plain bicorn with gold button, loop, dark green cockade. Offs., white plumes with crimson bases, silver-and-crimson tassels: NCOs, white plumes with crimson tips, white-and-crimson tassels (silver-and-crimson for sergeant majors); privates, dark green plumes, crimson bases, dark green-and-crimson tassels; hornists ('Habmondbläser'), dark green plumes with three equal crimson stripes incl. base, dark green tip.

The coat is described variously as 'green' or 'light green', but in Vol. IX, Pl. 3 of his *Uniformenkunde* Knötel shows a green which can only be called 'green, to dark green'. In the absence of a regimental history this matter is unlikely to be resolved. The coats were of infantry cut with crimson F shown at CLR, L, C, and shoulder straps; red TB with green hearts at intersections; green double-breasted W; green B (offs., buff); all ranks wore short knee-boots. White belts and pouch bandolier. Brown leather satchel on brown strap over right shoulder. Brass-hilted Hirschfänger, without strap, in brown sheath at waist. Sergeants and above wore gold-laced C and CLR, small gold epaulettes, white gauntlets; offs. wore white gloves.

Cavalry

Garde du Corps

Officers' court uniform Plain bicorn, silver star brooch, black cockade, white-over-crimson plume. Red coat, CF; light blue CLR, L, C, TB; silver BTN. White W, B. Silver right-hand aiguillette; high, cuffed boots; sword. *Officers' undress uniform* Coat dark blue, single-breasted, silver BTN and aiguillette. Hat, W, B, boots, sword as above. *Officers' service uniform* Hat, boots as above. Buff Kollet tunic; red C, edged silver; red CLR; buff TB; silver lace edging. Buff leather B, white knee cuffs; heavy cavalry sword, gold basket hilt, black sheath.

Other Ranks Bicorn with silver loop, white-below-crimson plume. Kollet as offs., but edging white with two red stripes. B as offs.; red waist sash; red sabretasche, red and white lace edging, crowned 'LL' cypher in brass. White leather pouch and bandolier, edged red and white; brass pouch badge. Heavy cavalry sword, brass basket hilt, black sheath furnished with brass.

Husaren-Corps

This was more of a gendarmerie force than a line regiment for field operations. White Flügelmütze, no peak; at front top a red rosette over light blue cord loop, silver BTN; red and white cords; off's. rosette, cords mixed red/silver; plume black for ORs, white-over-crimson for offs. White dolman, red C, CLR; silver BTN; lace and edging silver or white, offs. or ORs. Light blue pelisse, silver BTN; silver lace, edging, grey fur trim (offs.), white lace, edging, black fur trim (ORs). Waist sash red and white (red and silver, offs.), with white (silver) barrels. Light blue B, white (silver) decoration at sides and thighs. Hungarian boots, silver trim, tassel. Light blue sabretasche, white (silver) edging, crowned gold 'LL'. White leather bandoliers for ORs, silver for offs.; brass-hilted sabre, black sheath furnished with brass.

Off's. undress uniform Bicorn as Garde du Corps; light blue surtout, single-breasted, mid-calf length, with silver BTN; red CLR, C; light blue CF. White B; plain Hungarian boots.

Regiment Chevaulegers (1806, Garde-Chevaulegers)

Black leather Kasket with vertical front plate cut-out at right side, edged gold, gold crowned 'LLX'. Black horse-hair crest front to back. Skulls of off's. helmets covered with leopard-skin turban. At right side, white plume (crimson base for offs.); under this red and silver tassels (offs.), rosette in squadron colours (unknown) for ORs.

Dark green tunic, red CLR; black L, C, CF; red TB. On each side CLR, horizontal white lace (silver for offs.), silver BTN at rear. White (silver for offs.) lace on L buttonholes, also two under each L; white (silver) chevrons on and above plain C, and on skirts, as cavalry ADCs, see above. At junction of TB, green patches for ORs, black with silver edges for offs.; red shoulder straps with white (silver) edges, centre stripe. Buff, double-breasted W, buff B; Hungarian boots, black tassel. Offs. carried gold-hilted sabres in black, gold-furnished sheaths; ORs, sabres with steel hilts and fittings. Offs. had silver bandoliers, ORs buff leather. *Off's. undress uniform* Bicorn; surtout in coat colours but single-breasted and without embroidery; white W, B; plain Hungarian boots.

In about 1806 the helmet was replaced by the high, domed style worn by Bavarian cavalry. A false, curved front plate was added, with new cypher of crowned 'L'. Black woollen 'sausage' crest for ORs, corporals; sergeants and above wore black bearskin crests. On the left side was a black plume with a red base, above a red-within-white cockade. In 1806 the coat came to be worn with the lapels closed to the waist.

Trumpeters were apparently distinguished by

Colour-bearer of Hessen-Kassel Landwehr, 1813 – from 'Freiwilligen 1813'. Dark blue Litewka, silver buttons, silver edging to collar and cuffs denoting senior NCO. Facings are crimson, indicating either 1st or 3rd Bn. – see text. The colour is red, with blue shield, silver cross inscribed 'Mit Gott für Fürst und Vaterland', and gold wreath, corner rays, crown and tip. The black pike has a gold shoe. The shako cover is black with a white Landwehr Cross, the greatcoat and breeches are grey, the belts black and the pack brown calf-skin. Just visible under the rolled greatcoat at front right of the belt is a brown pistol holster.

Elector Wilhelm I of Hessen, 1806. A trace of triumph is perhaps visible in the countenance of this ruler; he had tried for years to achieve this status, investing enormous sums in an unsuccessful show of pomp in 1803 designed to impress the Imperial representatives in Frankfurt. Nominated an Elector at last, he was 'abolished' by Napoleon following the battles of Jena and Auerstädt. (After an engraving in the Staatsbibliothek Kassel)

red plumes; no lace to L buttonholes; white L edging. It is assumed they rode greys. Brass trumpets, red and white cords.

Harness was black with silver fittings; the round portmanteau was green, edged red at the ends. The shabraque was green, edged with white lace having a narrow black central stripe. In the rear corners was the crowned cypher in white; front corners, initially plain, had a white symbol added in 1812.

Artillery

As for line infantry, with dark blue coats, black F, gold BTN, red TB. Majors and above had gold laced buttonholes; all offs. had wide, scalloped gold HL, gold star brooch, gold aiguillettes. ORs' hats edged white. White W, B. Straight sword in place of inf. sabre.

Train

Offs. – plain bicorn, silver star brooch; single-breasted dark blue coat, CF; red C, CLR; white TB, W, B; silver BTN; high boots, sword. Wagenmeister (equivalent to NCO) – silver HL, BTN, and above BTN red-within-white NCO pompon; dark blue coat, two rows BTN, lapels closed over; dark blue W, B; red CLR, C, edged silver; red TB; high boots.

Uniform Changes After 1792

1803 Musketeer offs. received white-over-red plumes; Füsilier offs. had no scalloped HL. Spontoons and halberds were discarded.

1804 NCOs received coat-colour shoulder straps.

1805 Füsilier-Bns. received lightweight Prussian Nothardt muskets.

1806 *August:* The state became a Grand Duchy. All waistcoats changed from white to dark blue (green for Füsiliers). Black cockades were changed to red-within-white from 12 July. Ors received blue (or green) forage caps piped and tasselled in regimental facing colour. From June to September each year winter legwear of blue cloth breeches and black gaiters was changed to long white linen trousers worn loose over black half-gaiters. *December:* Instead of being worn on a right shoulder bandolier, the pack was fitted with two white straps and worn high on the back; for this reason the coat acquired a right shoulder strap. The pigtail was abolished. Musketeers received captured Prussian muskets. On field service officers were permitted a blue 'Überrock' – lit., overcoat – blue breeches (both green for Füsiliers) with Suvorov boots, and plain bicorns. After some unfortunate incidents during the battle of Jena, officers now wore a red plume with a black base, to avoid confusion with Prussian officers. Officers and ORs lost the hat edging.

1809 Regiment Gross- und Erbprinz re-organised, and subsequently re-badged, on French lines. The Füsilier-Bn. changed their green coats for dark blue with regimental facings and buttons but white hunting-horns on turnbacks. French infantry shako began to replace bicorn for other ranks, with white metal shield bearing Hessian lion under red-within-white cockade held by white loop and button. Chinscales were white metal for the Leib-Regt., black edged with facing colour for other regiments. Black plume for parades. Above cockade was a company pompon beneath a red pompon with a red tuft. NCOs' plumes tipped red, officers' plumes with red base. officers retained bicorn until 1816. Company pompons were: 1st, white; 2nd, black; 3rd, blue; 4th, red; 5th, white-over-yellow; 6th, black-over-white; 7th, blue-over-white; 8th, red-over-white. Sabre straps were in company colours. French rank badges, service chevrons, and élite company badges were introduced. Prussian muskets began to be replaced by French 1777 muskets and by captured Austrian weapons for musketeers. Sabres were now worn on a bandolier over the right shoulder instead of the waist belt. Officers' coat turnbacks were in coat-colour instead of red; the coat was closed across the chest and the sash worn over it.

1810 ORs' shoulder straps replaced by blue fringeless contre-epaulettes edged in facing colour for privates, in white and facing colour for NCOs.

1811 Austrian muskets replaced the Füsiliers' Nothardt muskets.

1812 'Provisional Light Infantry Regiment' (see under Leib-Garde and Leib-Füsilier-Bns.) wore Leib-Garde-Regt. uniform with scarlet facings and silver buttons, and white hunting-horns on turn-backs. Officers carried curved sabres, and silver cartouches, on black bandoliers crossing on the chest. Shako chinscales were white metal. Belts were black until the unit became the Garde-Füsilier-Regt., then white.

1814 Regiment Prinz Emil raised; disbanded 1820; dark blue coat, pink facings, silver buttons. Contre-epaulettes replaced by straight-edged shoulder straps edged at sides and top in facing colour: Leib-Garde-Regt., red; Leib-Regt., light blue; Regt. Gross- und Erbprinz, yellow; Regt. Prinz Emil, pink.

All the foregoing details were theoretical; in practice such perfection was rarely achieved, particularly on campaign. An extract from the regimental history of the 118th Infantry (pp. 130–136) serves to show how the practicalities of life disrupted theoretical distinctions:

'On 19 August 1808 the Brigade Gross- und Erbprinz paraded in Gross-Gerau in order to be re-organised into a two-battalion regiment on French lines – each battalion of one grenadier, one voltigeur and four fusilier companies. This re-organisation took place there on 23 August under direction of the French General Boyer, especially sent from Mainz by Marshal Kellermann. To form the élite companies those men with most service were picked out from all twelve old companies. The tallest of these formed the two new grenadier companies and the shortest became the voltigeurs.'

Following this operation the new companies presented a dreadful military picture, with green-clad ex-Füsiliers mixed willy-nilly with blue-

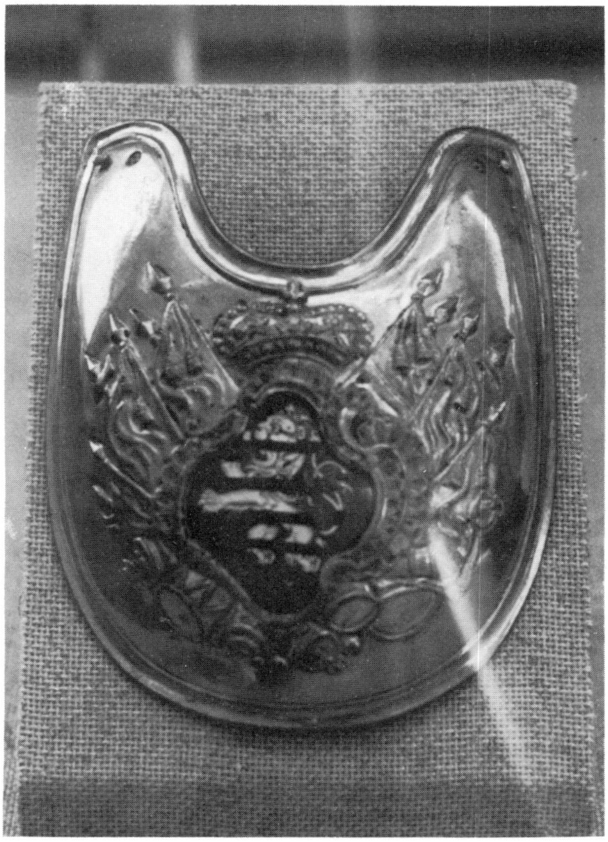

Gold Hessen-Kassel officer's gorget, *c*.1788; the centrepiece is blue with a red-and-white striped lion. (Schloss Friedrichstein Museum)

coated ex-line battalion men. There was no 'magic' instant issue of new uniforms, or of the red and green plumes, epaulettes and sabre knots for the élite companies. The motley regiment remained a thorn in the sartorial flesh for many weeks; and even after new uniforms were issued from French magazines they rapidly wore out during the strenuous summer campaign, and troops were reduced to making up their own trousers from requisitioned blue, brown or white cloth. Later in the campaign they even cut off their coat-tails in order to patch up the rest of their coats. In mid-August 1809 an officer of the regiment was sent back to Bayonne to draw new uniforms for the men from French magazines. He eventually returned with the very welcome new clothing to Segovia, where the bulk of the regiment then served, in late December 1809.

Campaign History Extracts

The March to Trieste and Croatia, 1796–97

Early in 1796 Britain asked that Ludwig X again provide a brigade of three battalions of infantry for service 'at any point' in the British possessions, continuing a long and successful tradition of Hessen-Darmstadt service to the British crown in America, Scotland, and on the continent of Europe. As the phrasing of this request might mean the fever-haunted death-trap of the West Indies all men enlisted in these battalions were volunteers, and most were in fact non-Hessians serving under Hessian officers. The brigade was mustered at Buchen in the Odenwald on 18 July 1796, with a strength of 2,248 all ranks. British rates of pay were paid, much higher than the domestic rates. It was expected that the brigade would march to Trieste and there take ship on Royal Navy vessels for the colonies; accordingly the Hessians christened it the 'Water-Brigade'.

The route of march lay through Swabia, Bavaria, Salzburg, Corinthia and Krain. The journey proved difficult, as despite the Landgraf's diplomatic efforts these states sometimes refused right of access when the brigade reached their frontiers. Desertion was also high, particularly among the 'foreigners'; 333 men had deserted by the time the column reached Ljubljana on 10 September and halted to rest. Many others had fallen out from sickness, and on 1 October the all-ranks duty strength was only 1,843.

Due to the unfavourable shift in the balance of naval power in the Mediterranean, the Royal Navy never appeared to embark them. On 29 December Oberst von Stosch, the brigade commander, received orders to place himself under command of the Austrian Feldzeugmeister Alvinzi. Due to their lack of field equipment – the British had only rented horses and wagons for a march originally intended to take them to embarkation for foreign service – the Hessians served as garrison troops, two battalions in Trieste and the light battalion at Rijeka (Fiume), from March 1797. On 20 March the Trieste battalions were also withdrawn to Rijeka when Napoleon pushed Erzherzog Karl's Austrians over the Tagliamento and Isonso rivers.

Early in April the Hessians were withdrawn once again, two battalions to Karlstadt in Croatia and the light battalion to Neustadtel in Krain. On 26 August 1797 Stosch received orders from England to return his troops to Darmstadt as quickly as possible. The brigade marched out on

Further examples of grenadier cap plates worn by unidentified Hessen-Kassel regiments, 1785–1803. These small plates would have been worn on the Austrian-style bearskin; both are white metal, the lower example bearing the crowned 'WL' cypher. (Schloss Friedrichstein Museum)

22 October, but despite buying horses and wagons to transport their many sick, numbers of these unfortunates had to be left behind in local hospitals. Darmstadt was reached on 15 December, and most of the serviceable soldiers were 'beurlaubt' – furloughed – only about 200 per battalion being retained.

Glimpses of the Peninsular War

French generals' bulletins to Paris from the Peninsula were heavy with praise for the French regiments involved, but frequently omitted mention of the valiant services rendered by their allies, the German units of the Confederation of the Rhine. An example is a report from Marshal Mortier concerning the battle of Ocaña on 19 November 1809. The Hessian Regiment Gross- und Erbprinz, one of many vassal contingents which served with the French army in this engagement, had one officer killed and four wounded, and approximately 70 men killed and wounded. Mortier's report to Paris stung General von Schaeffer, then commander of the Hessians in Spain, to write the following indignant letter to his sovereign:

'The progress which the war in Andalusia makes is a result of the battle of Ocaña in which the Germans as a whole and in particular the Regiment Gross- und Erbprinz played such a vital part. It is thus even more insulting that the part played by the French is so emphasized while the Germans receive a purely superficial mention. Some French regiments are lionized, who never even fired a shot on that day. This is particularly the case with the 88^{e} de Ligne, of which Marshal Mortier says: "It stood on the left wing, and distinguished itself". I can assure Your Highness on my honour, that during the battle this regiment was 400 paces behind my brigade, never fired a shot, had no wounded, and only came up in line with my formation when the battle was over!'

After this battle the German division was allotted the despised task of escorting Spanish prisoners; this was too much for von Schaeffer, who promptly tendered his resignation in the face of so gross an insult.

The Hessians achieved a first-class fighting reputation among their enemies, the Spanish

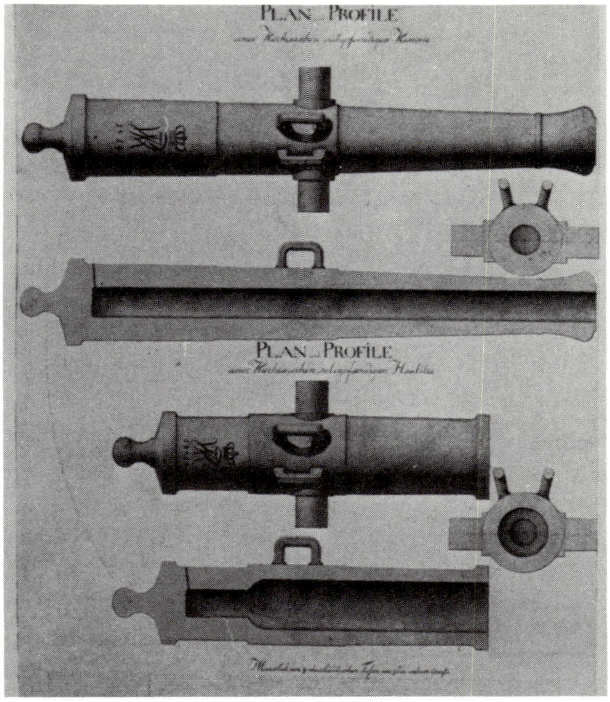

Hessen-Kassel cannon and howitzer, cast in 1814. Top to bottom: plan view, 6-pdr. cannon, with end view and cutaway section; similar views of 7-pdr. howitzer. The princely cypher 'WK' may be seen, with the date of casting, at the touch-hole. The narrow breech section of the howitzer barrel held the propellant charge, inserted by hand; the projectile was then placed on top of this. (After a diagram drawn in 1819)

guerrilleros, in the Toledo area. One officer was told by Spanish peasants that a notorious guerillero chief, Camillo, had been waiting in ambush near them with 200 men. On being informed that a small detachment marching along the road from Almonacid were 'Hessos', Camillo turned to his officers with the words: 'Gentlemen, we will leave them alone. They sell their lives for more than they are worth.'

The bitter nature of the war between the Spanish population and the invaders is horribly underlined, however, by an incident which took place on the road from Burgos to Madrid in December 1808, just after the Hessians had entered Spain:

'On 28 December Grenadier Schneider was ordered to march with a cart on w ich were loaded the baggage and Schneider's heavily-pregnant wife. (This was between Baitrago and St. Antonia.) The cart had fallen about 200 paces behind the battalion when suddenly several shots were heard. They rushed back only to find

Two Hessen-Kassel infantry tunics, *c.*1790–1806. They are dark blue with red facings and white lace, and may possibly be of the Regiment Prinz Karl. The coat with the higher collar would be of the 1806 period, the other of an earlier date and with two red shoulder straps. (Schloss Friedrichstein Museum)

both the grenadier and his wife murdered, hideously mutilated and lying in the road. The woman's stomach had been slit open and her breasts cut off; Schneider had been disfigured in an even worse manner which it is better not to relate.' (From the regimental history of Infantry Regiment Nr. 118.)

The regimental history of the Regiment Gross- und Erbprinz contains an extensive account of the siege, storm and fall of Badajoz – the vital key to the door from Portugal into Spain – and considerable space is devoted to clearing the regiment's honour, besmirched by a dubious report by a French staff officer.

The fortress fell after bitter fighting on the night of 6–7 April 1812. British and Portuguese losses are given as 72 officers and 963 ORs killed, 333 officers and 3,581 ORs wounded, and one officer and 62 ORs missing. Exact casualties among the defenders were never established, but it is known that of the original 4,500 of all ranks some 2,500 were taken prisoner on 7 April.

After the town walls had been breached and the surviving defenders were falling back on the castle, the attack was concentrated on this last bastion, which was held by the Hessians. Seeing that the situation was becoming critical, Oberst Köhler, commanding the Gross- und Erbprinz, sent two Underadjutants to Governor Phillipon on the evening of 5 April to report the serious developments. When they eventually found the general he was in the act of leaving the castle, together with his staff and several mule-loads of effects, to flee over the river to the safety of Fort Christobal! The castle fell about 24 hours later.

During their subsequent captivity in Britain a report of the exact sequence of events during the storming and fall of Badajoz was compiled, and signed at Llanfylling on 5 August 1812, by three colonels, five battalion commanders, and 42 company officers of the former garrison. This report, reflecting nothing but credit upon the Regiment Gross- und Erbprinz, was handed in to the French War Ministry, filed, and forgotten. In 1825, however, Col. Lamare – who had been Phillipon's chief of staff, and was one of the officers who made his way to Fort Christobal 24 hours before the relevant events – published his own account of the fall of the castle, in which the blame for its loss was firmly attributed to the dubious loyalty of the Hessians. Lamare's book was reprinted, uncorrected, in 1837.

One could be forgiven for dismissing this dispute as a case of 'six of one and half-a-dozen of the other' were it not for the existence of an interesting document discovered after his death among Oberst Köhler's papers. The original was handed to the Hessian State Archives; and a copy was sent to M. Thiers, author of the widely read *History of the Consulate and the Empire*, who had repeated Lamare's slander, and even embroidered upon it, in Vol. 13 of that work. The document read:

'Nous, général de Division, baron de l'empire, gouverneur de Badajoz, certifions, que depuis le commencement du siége de cette place jusqu'a la fin, le régiment de Hesse-Darmstadt, qui faisit partie de la garnison, s'est toujours comporté de la maniére la plus brave; il a, comme tous les autres

bataillons, fait preuve de valeur et de bravour; on ne peut que se louer de la conduite de ce régiment, etc.
Lisbonne le 19 Avril 1812

Phillipon'

Impartial accounts of the defence of Badajoz may be found in the British works *Journal of the Sieges Undertaken by the Allies in Spain 1811–12*, by Lt.Col. Jones of the Royal Engineers, who commanded the siege works there; and *Memoirs of Lieutenant-General Sir Thomas Picton*, whose division actually stormed the castle.

Hessen-Darmstadt Campaign Summary

1792 Storm of Frankfurt am Main (Chevaulegers only)
1793 Upper Rhine
1794 Low Countries
1795 Upper Rhine
1796 Trieste, Croatia (infantry only); Upper Rhine (Regt. Erbprinz only)
1806 Battle of Jena (Garde-Füsiliers only)
1807 Campaign in Prussia and Poland, January-August
1808–12 Campaign in Spain (Regt. Gross- und Erbprinz only) incl. battle of Talavera and siege and fall of Badajoz
1809 Campaign in Germany and Austria
1812 Russia (all regts. except Gross- und Erbprinz)
1813 Campaign in Saxony (all regts. except Gross- und Erbprinz)
1814 Campaign in France
1815 Upper Rhine

Colours and Standards

Infantry Colours

From 1790 to 1813 the 1st Company of each battalion carried an Avancirfahne or sovereign's colour, and the 4th Company a Retirirfahne or battalion colour. From 1813 only one per battalion was carried: the regimental Leibfahne by the 1st Company (Leib-Kompagnie), 1st Bn., and a Bataillonsfahne by the other battalions.

On 6 April 1790 Landgraf Ludwig X presented new colours to most existing regiments; painted on silk, they were fragile and thus relatively frequently replaced. Designs of Avancir and Retirirfahnen were basically similar apart from colour. All bore the red-and-white striped Hessian lion with sword and crown on a central light blue disc, surrounded by a green laurel wreath tied at the bottom with red ribbon. Across the top a scroll bore 'PRO PATRIA' under a golden Landgraf's crown. In each corner a smaller wreath and crown enclosed 'LLX'; centrally on each side was a silver-and-red flaming grenade. The cypher appeared on the pierced golden spearhead finial; a silver-and-red cravat hung down to the halfway point of the colour. The cloth, 1.3m square, was nailed to a regimentally-coloured pike with 40–50 round gold nails. The Avancirfahnen, and the Retirirfahnen of the Leib-Garde, were all white; other Retirirfahnen

Cavalry weapons. The carbine is of unidentified manufacture, but probably Hanoverian, pre-1803 (due to pinning of stock to barrel, rather than use of ring clamps); the pistol, of French style, was probably from the Solingen arsenal. (Schloss Friedrichstein Museum)

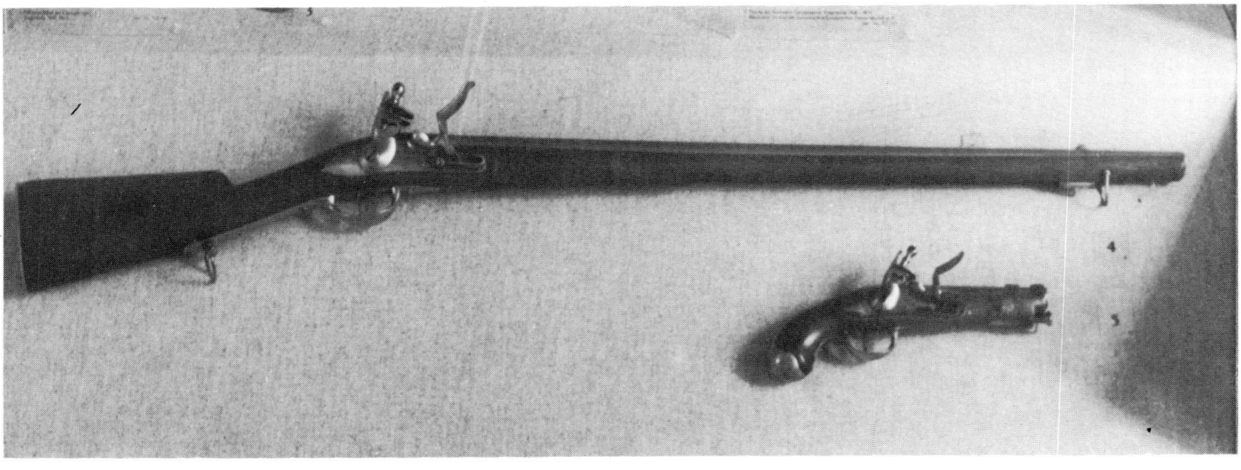

Hessen-Darmstadt Chevaulegers officer, 1790–1808 – a plate in the regimental history. See Plate A.

usually showed regimental facings in a saltire. When furled the colours were protected by black oilcloth covers with brass caps bearing regimental designations.

From 1803 only musketeer battalions carried colours. On 12 March 1804 the Regiment Erbprinz received the following new colours: one Avancirfahne, white ground, black-and-yellow halved saltire; three Retirirfahnen, black ground, yellow saltire, silver-and-red grenades; black pikes.

Despite Ludwig's elevation to Grand Duke in 1806 the colour remained unchanged until 1814, when new painted colours were presented to all regiments re-raised at that time. Central designs were largely unchanged; the crown design was that of a Grand Duke, scrolls now bore 'GOTT EHRE VATERLAND' (God, Honour, Fatherland), and the cypher in all positions was a gold crowned 'L'. The colours were 1.12m high by 1.09m wide; the 2.98m black pikes had 28.7cm gold finials, and silver-and-red cords and tassels reaching about halfway down the colour. Oilcloth cover caps bore the cypher and regimental title.

The Regiment Gross- und Erbprinz took to Spain in August 1808 the Retirirfahne of the 1st Bn. and the Avancirfahne of the 2nd Bn.; both were captured at the fall of Badajoz by Private George Hatton of the 4th Foot, and were laid up in the hall of the Royal Hospital, Chelsea. Subsequently the pikes and the few tatters of cloth then surviving were passed to the Regimental Museum of the King's Own Border Regiment (4th, 34th and 55th Foot).

The Regiments Landgraf's 2nd Bn. lost its colour at Wagram during bitter fighting for the key village of Aderklaa on 6 July 1809.

Cavalry Standards

The Chevaulegers carried no standards. The Garde du Corps carried from 1770 a silver standard fringed with gold, bearing a blue saltire. In the centre was the great crest of Landgraf Ludwig IX supported by lions and under an array of crested helmets. Below the crest was the star of the Order of the Black Eagle, above military trophies. In each corner crowned wreaths enclosed a reversed double 'L' cypher, repeated on the gold spearhead finial of the dark blue staff. This standard was taken over in 1860 by the newly-raised 2tes Dragoner-Regiment (Leib-Dragoner-Regiment) Nr. 24, who carried it until disbandment after the First World War.

Colours Presented in 1790

Regt.	*Avancirfahnen*	*Retirirfahnen*
Leib-Garde	One. White ground & saltire, white pike.	Three. White ground & saltire; silver & red grenades; white pikes.
Landgraf	One. White ground, halved red & black saltire, brown pike.	Three. Black ground, red saltire & grenades, brown pikes
Erbprinz (Feld-bataillon)	One. White ground, halved pink & black saltire, brown pike.	One. Black ground, pink saltire, red grenades, brown pike.

Regt. & date of presentation	*Colours presented in 1814* *Avancirfahnen*	*Retirirfahnen*
Leib-Garde 8.2.14	Two. White ground & saltire, black pikes.	—
Garde-Füsilier-Regt. 8.2.14	Two. White ground, red saltire, black pikes.	—
Leib-Regt.[1] 9.2.14	One (1st Bn.). White ground, halved pink & black saltire, black pike.	One (2nd Bn.). Black ground, pink saltire, black pike.
Prinz Emil[2] 27.3.14	One (1st Bn.). White ground, halved blue & black saltire, black pike.	One (2nd Bn.). Black ground, blue saltire, black pike.
Gross- und Erbprinz 31.7.14	One (1st Bn.). White ground, halved black & yellow saltire, black pike.	One (2nd Bn.). Black ground, yellow saltire, black pike.

[1]These colours originally intended for the Regt. Prinz Emil; as the Leib-Regt.'s own colours were not ready by march-out date they received these, which were available, and carried them until after the First World War.

[2]Prinz Emil subsequently received the colours originally intended for the Leib-Regt., and carried them until after the First World War.

Hessen-Kassel Uniforms, 1792

Line Infantry – General Notes

Musketeer and Fusilier Officers Scalloped BTN-colour HL, BTN, loop and brooch on tricorn hat with black cockade, white plume with red (crimson?) base, silver and crimson tassels. Dark blue coat, BTN-colour lace, long skirts. Silver gorget on black ribbon, gold trophies around

Hessen-Darmstadt: Prinz Emil as General of the Cavalry. This portrait, a plate in the regimental history, shows the uniform details of the period 1808–15. The British influence is most marked.

Another plate from the regimental history shows Oberst von Münchingen, wearing the coat lapels folded across – a common practice, especially in winter. The bandolier plate bears the crowned cypher 'L', dating the plate to 1808–15. Among the decorations at the throat the Legion d'Honneur may be seen.

Hessen-Darmstadt infantry uniforms, 1807–09. Both are shown in field service marching order, with the calfskin pack in the 'new' position – on the back instead of slung on the right hip. By this date the pigtail had been cut off, and the white hat edging removed; on top of the hat was a company-coloured pompon – see text for details. Left, the Leib-Regiment, in dark blue faced with light blue; right, the Leib-Garde-Regiment (or 'Leibgarde-Regt.' – styles vary) in dark blue faced with red. The Füsilier battalions wore green coats. (After Knötel, Vol. XIV, No. 15 – by kind permission W. Spemann Verlag, Franck'sche Verlagshandlung, Stuttgart)

crowned blue disc with cypher 'WL'. Silver and crimson waist sash worn over W; gilt-hilted Degen sword, brown sheath, silver and crimson knot. Spontoon with silver and gilt decorated blade bearing black 'WL'. Long black gaiters with regimentally-coloured BTN. White gauntlets. Hair powdered, curled and queued to small of back; clean-shaven.

Grenadier Officers As above except: black bearskin caps with regimental front plate, bag and tassel; white plume, crimson tip. Short muskets with broad, decorated bayonets bearing the cypher replaced spontoons, and sabres replaced swords. White waist belt over W, with front central small cartouche with silver lid bearing cypher on crowned disc within trophies.

Senior Musketeer NCOs Narrow BTN-colour HL, except where noted specifically; crimson-and-white pompon, tassels. BTN-colour lace on short-skirted coat. White gauntlets. Halberd. Brown cane, gilt knob, black cord. Red and white sabre knot. Hair as offs.; no moustaches. *Junior Musketeer NCOs* Privates' uniform, but with red and white sabre knot; brown cane with black cord.

Grenadier NCOs As musketeers, but grenadier cap, and small black pouch worn front centre of white waist belt over the W. Red and white cap pompon; BTN-colour HL, vertically. Moustaches.

Füsilier NCOs As musketeers, but regimental fusilier caps.

Musketeer Privates Tricorn, regimental BTN and HL, red-and-white pompon, tassels. Dark blue coat with F at C, L, CLR; red TB (except Regt. Knyphausen, white). Regimental W, B. Black gaiters, regimental BTN. Red musket slings. Brown hide pack slung at left hip, white strap. Plain black cartridge pouch, white bandolier; Prussian brass-hilted sabre, white fist strap, brown sheath, on white waist belt; both have brass frame buckles. Hair as offs.; clean-shaven.

Grenadier privates As above except: black bearskin cap; regimental plate, bag, tassel; red-tipped white plume; moustaches. *Füsilier privates* As musketeers except regimental fusilier caps.

Guards Infantry As for respective ranks in line infantry except: white/silver scalloped HL all ranks musketeers; white/silver right-hand aiguillette, all ranks; yellow W, B; brass or silver pouch flap badge of crowned eight-point star enclosing cypher, and flaming grenade in each corner, flames to centre.

Drummers Negroes in some regiments; wore turbans. Otherwise musketeer, grenadier, fusilier headgear. Sleeves decorated with seven down-pointing chevrons of special lace below dark blue swallows' nests edged and decorated with same lace. Drum bandoliers white, edged with relevant lace; brown sticks; brass drums bearing crowned, rampant Hessian lion amid trophies; white cords, hoops diagonally striped red and white. No aprons. In some regiments drummers' lapels edged with lace.

Drum majors No definite information found; presumably NCOs' distinctions with lace and swallows' nests.

Regimental Distinctions, 1792

Guards Infantry:

Leib-Grenadier-Garde

Poppy red F; silver BTN; yellow W, B (white,

1801). White plumes, offs. with red base, ORs with red tip. Silver grenadier cap plates. Yellow pikes. Drummers, negroes, wore white lace with repeated crimson 'WL' cypher.

Garde-Grenadiere

'Royal red' (*sic*) F; silver BTN; coat lace tasselled. Yellow W, B (white, 1801). Musketeers had silver-fronted mitre caps; on plate, red-and-white

Hessen-Darmstadt artillery in Germany and Austria, 1809, during the Aspern-Wagram campaign. The gunners have dark blue uniforms faced with black, piped red; officers' facings were unpiped. Note rank distinctions in pattern of plumes – see text. The gunner at left wears a buff bricole for gun-handling. Two drivers in the background – at this period, having semi-civilian status – wear light blue coats faced red with silver buttons, and red hat pompons. The artillery equipment was painted grey with black metal fittings. (After Knötel, Vol. VII, No. 22 – by kind permission W. Spemann Verlag, Franck'sche Verlagshandlung, Stuttgart)

Hessen-Darmstadt, musketeer private of the Leibgarde-Regiment, 1808. This plate is dated by the lack of pigtail, and the plain bicorn with a company tuft or pompon; dark blue coat faced with red, white lace, silver buttons. (After Weiland)

striped Hessian lion over gold 'WL' on blue disc; silver headband, yellow backing, white lace, yellow tassel. Grenadier bearskins had silver plate, yellow bag, white lace and tassel. Yellow pikes. Negro drummers as Leib-Grenadier-Garde.

Line Infantry:

Leib-Infanterie-Regiment

1803, Kürfurst.

Yellow F, silver BTN, white W, B. Drummers' lace crimson, edged white.

Regiment von Kospoth (Füsiliers)

1801, von Biesenrodt; 1805, Kürprinz.

White F, silver BTN, no coat lace; white W, buff B. Fusilier cap had buff headpiece, brass straps and top grenade, plate details unclear. Grenadiers had black bearskin, buff bag, white lace and tassel, red-tipped white plume. White pikes. Drummers' lace, red-and-white dice.

Regiment Erbprinz

1803, Kürprinz; 1805, von Wurmb; 1813, vacant von Wurmb, then Prinz von Solms-Braunfels. Crimson F, silver BTN, offs.' lace removed *c.*1792. No plumes; hat pompons quartered crimson/white for all NCOs, ORs. Grenadier caps had brass plates, crimson bags, white trim and tassel, red-tipped white plume. Black pikes. Drummers' lace crimson, edged white.

Regiment Prinz Karl

1805, Landgraf Karl.

Field poppy red F, edged white; gold BTN; white W. No plumes; gold/white HL, pompoms white-within-red. Brass grenadier cap plates with rampant lion; red bag, white lace and tassel, red-tipped white plume. Black pikes. Drummers' lace crimson, edged white.

Füsilier-Regiment von Lossberg

1799, von Linsingen; 1805, von Biesenrodt; 1813, von Biesenrodt – one bn. only, attached Garde-Grenadiere as Flügel-Grenadier-Bataillon.

Orange F, gold BTN, no lace, white W. Fusilier caps had brass plate, details unclear; black headpiece, brass strips and top grenade. Grenadier bearskins black, brass plate, details unclear; orange bag, white trim and tassel, red-tipped white plume. White pikes. Drummers' lace dark blue with red zig-zag, all edged orange.

Regiment von Ditfurth

1792, von Hanstein; disbanded 1795.

Yellow F, gold BTN; gold/white lace under lapels only. HL: offs. gold, NCOs none, ORs white. No plumes; pompons halved red and white. Grenadiers wore black bearskins, brass plate, details unclear; yellow bag, white trim and tassel, red-tipped white plume. Black pikes. Drummers' lace crimson, edged white.

Light Infantry

Uniforms as line except where shown below:

Jäger-Bataillon (or Feld-Jäger-Corps)

Green coats, crimson F, silver BTN; white right-hand aiguillettes. White W, B, belts. Green cockade, white-and-green plume; tassels silver-and-crimson, offs. and senior NCOs; green-and-crimson, ORs and junior NCOs. NCOs and ORs carried large brown leather satchel on brown strap, rifles, sword bayonets. Offs. carried sword only, and wore high, cuffed boots with buckle-on steel spurs. Hornists replaced drummers: brass horns with white-and-crimson cords; green swallows' nests with crimson lace edged silver. By 1794 all ranks wore silver epaulettes, both shoulders.

Leichtes Infanterie-Bataillon Lentz

Raised 1788 from Feld-Jäger-Corps and from among small men in infantry and cavalry. Headdress unknown. Green coats, scarlet CLR, L, C, TB. Silver BTN, epaulettes; white W, B. Initially with four companies, reduced to two, 1792. Provided a cadre for a two-company 'Füsilier-Bataillon', 1793, which re-combined with parent regt. in 1795, title changing to Füsilier-Bataillon von Prüschenck. 1799, reinforced by the two depot companies of Regts. Prinz Karl and von Kospoth, the new four-company battalion taking name of commander, Major Marquand. 1806, title changed to von Todenwarth, and later disbanded.

Füsilier-Bataillon Schlotheim

Raised 1799 from the four depot companies of Regts. Garde-Grenadiere, Leib-Infanterie, Erbprinz and von Linsingen; disbanded 1806. Headdress unknown. Green coats, 'royal red' CLR, L, C, TB; silver BTN, epaulettes; white W, B.

Garrison Infantry:

Uniforms as line except where shown below:

Garnisons-Regiment Köhler

Offs.: Bicorn with narrow gold HL, black cockade, gold loop and BTN, no plume. Dark blue coat, L, CF; white CLR, C; red TB. White W, B. Gold gorget, crowned cypher within trophies. White gauntlets; black spontoon. *Musketeer NCOs*: As line but with coat as offs., gold edged C, CF; red-and-white portepee; white gauntlets; black halberd. *Musketeers*: As NCOs without gold lace; white HL, red-within-white pompons; white belts, sabre straps. *Grenadiers:* As musketeers except brass cap plate with lion between grenades, dark blue backing, white lace and band, black-and-white pompon. White sabre strap with black tassel. Moustaches. *Drummers*: Dark blue swallows' nests edged and striped with red lace with white central stripe. Same lace edged C, CF. Brass drums, red-and-white hoops.

Garnisons-Regiment von Porbeck

As Köhler except: red C, CLR; grenadier cap headband red, HL yellow, white cloth backing, black-and-white pompon. Drummers' lace dark blue, white central stripe.

Garnisons-Regiment Matthias

Red CLR, C; gold BTN; white W, B. ORs' hat pompon red-within-white. Grenadier cap with brass plate of rampant lion, red band, white HL, dark blue cloth backing, black-and-white pompon. Drummers' lace crimson, edged red.

Garnisons-Regiment von Colson

Crimson CLR, C; gold BTN; white W, B. ORs' hat pompons red-within-white; white HL. Grenadier caps had brass plate, design unclear; crimson band, yellow cloth backing, white, HL, black-and-white pompon. Drummers' lace crimson, white central stripe.

Garnisons-Regiment von Knoblauch

Yellow CLR, C, W, B; silver BTN, red TB. ORs' hat as von Colson. Grenadier caps had brass plate with rampant lion, yellow band, white

Hessen-Darmstadt troops, 1811 – from the Augsburger Bilder. Left to right: *Trooper, Chevaulegers* – black helmet, yellow metal fittings; green coat with black lapels, collar tabs and cuffs; red collar, shoulder straps and turn-backs; green breeches with red piping; buff leather, steel sheath. *Musketeer, Leib-Regt.* – dark blue coat faced light blue, white lace, silver buttons; black plume, red-and-white cockade, silver chinscales. *Musketeer, Leibgarde-Regt.* – as central figure but red facings, red-and-white pompon. The absence of shako shields is unexplained.

The helmet plate of this pickelhaube of the Infanterie-Regiment Nr. 116 (the Garde-Füsiliere and I. Leib-Füsiliere during the Napoleonic era) shows the retention of traditional German state heraldry in the military trappings of 1914: note the 'striped' effect of the Hessian lion motif. (Wehrhistorisches Museum, Rastatt)

cloth backing, black HL, white pompon. Drummers' lace light blue, white central stripe.

Land-Grenadier-Regiment As for Garrison Infantry except as follows:

Offs.: Silver gorget, blue disc bearing gold cypher under crown amid gold trophies. Three pairs gold lace loops on L, one pair under L, three on CF. Red C, TB; dark blue CLR. Buff W, B. Black spontoons. *Füsilier NCOs*: No loops on L, CF; gold-laced C, CF. Brass-fronted mitre caps, red band, dark blue cloth backing, white HL, red-and-white pompon. Red-and-white portepee; black halberds. *Füsiliers*: White cap pompon; red shoulder strap (left), white sabre strap. *Grenadiers*: Black Austrian-style fur caps, small brass plate, red-over-white plume. Red shoulder strap (left); white sabre strap, black tassel. Moustaches.

Drummers: Headgear as company. ORs' uniform with dark blue swallows' nests edged with crimson lace, edged white; this lace on C, CF. Brass drums, red-and-white hoops.

Kreis-Regiment Heymel

This was Hessen-Kassel's standing contribution to the military effort of the Holy Roman Empire. Uniform of garrison infantry style with red CLR, C, L, TB, W, B; gold BTN. Brown offs.' spontoons. Grenadiers had Austrian caps, brass plate with cypher within trophies, red-over-white plume; white sabre strap, black tassel; moustaches. Drummers' lace light blue, yellow centre stripe.

Invaliden-Bataillon Beck

Garrison infantry style uniform, red CLR, L, C, TB, silver BTN. Dark blue W, B. No grenadiers; no HL for ORs or NCOs, the latter distinguished only by black halberds, white gloves, red-and-white portepee. Offs.' spontoons black. Drummers' lace crimson, edged white.

The Depot Battalions

No details of uniform are known; staff and recruits probably wore the uniforms of the parent regiments, as follows:

1st Bn. von Porbeck – depot unit for Leib-Grenadier-Garde, Garde-Grenadiere, Erbprinz, Prinz Karl regiments. *2nd Bn. von Schallern* – depot unit for Leib-Infanterie, von Lossberg, von Kospoth and von Hanstein regiments. (These units only existed 1792–95.)

Artillery

Uniform of line infantry style. Crimson CLR, C, L, TB, gold BTN. Buff W, B, offs.' gauntlets. Offs.' HL gold; no plume; no gorget; black spontoon. NCOs' HL narrow gold, gold BTN, no loop, white-within-crimson pompon; gold lace edging to C, CF; red-and-white portepee, white belts. Gunners' HL white, white-within-crimson pompons; white sabre strap and bandolier with brass picker equipment. Drummers' lace crimson, edged yellow. Dark blue swallows' nests edged and decorated with this lace, which also edged L, C, drum bandolier. Seven chevrons of lace point down on sleeves. Usual drum.

The Land-Regiments

Raised in 1794, and named after the major towns around which they were recruited, these wore line infantry uniform with unlaced dark blue coats:

Hessen-Darmstadt: Officer, Chevaulegers, 1790-1803

A

Hessen-Darmstadt:
1. Private, 3rd Coy., Leichtes Infanterie-Bataillon, 1790
2. Oberst, Artillery, 1792
3. Hornist, Füsilier-Bataillon, Brigade Landgraf, 1803

Hessen-Darmstadt:
1. Officer, Leib-Regiment, 1807-09
2. Trooper, Garde-du-Corps, 1809
3. Sergeant, Foot Artillery, 1809

C

Hessen-Darmstadt:
1. Corporal, Grenadier Coy., Regt.'Gross-und Erbprinz'; Spain, 1809
2. Officer, Leib-Regiment, 1812
3. Trooper, Garde-Chevaulegers, 1812

D

Hessen-Darmstadt:
1. Officer, 1st Coy., Freiwillige Jäger, 1813-14
2. Officer, Leib-Garde-Regiment, 1814
3. Private, Regiment 'Prinz Emil', 1814

Hessen-Kassel:
1. NCO, Füsiliers, Leib-Regiment, 1792
2. Officer, Hussars, 1792
3. Drummer, Regiment Garde, 1792

F

Hessen-Kassel:
1. Officer, Light Infantry, Kur-Hessian Legion, 1809
2. Trumpeter, Karabiniers, 1792
3. Officer of Grenadiers, Garde-Grenadiere, 1792

Hessen-Kassel:
1. Officer, Regiment 'Landgraf Karl', 1814
2. NCO of Jägers, 1814
3. NCO, Horse Artillery, 1816

H

Regt.	*CLR, C*	*BTN*	*W, B*	
Cassel	Field poppy red	Silver	White	(4 Bns. 1794, reduced to 2 Bns., 1795)
Marburg	Yellow	Silver	Yellow	(3 Bns. 1794, 1 Bn. 1795)
Eschwege	Crimson	Silver	White	(4 Bns. 1794, 2 Bns. 1795)

Infanterie-Ordinärfahne, Hessen-Kassel, *c.*1792. This design of colour had been carried by the Hessians in the War of American Independence. Apparently each company in the regiment apart from the Leib-Kompagnie carried such a colour, but only very incomplete details of the colours carried by each regiment have survived. Sometimes the corner 'flames' were of the same colour as the ground, sometimes of contrasting colours. The central disc was blue, the lion red-and-white, the grass green, the grenades and laurel wreaths silver, the crowns gold with red cushions, and the scroll pink with a gold inscription 'NESCIT PERICULA' – 'Regardless of danger'. (After Thalmann)

Regt.	*CLR, C*	*BTN*	*W, B*	
Hersfeld	White	Silver	White	(2 Bns. 1794, 1 Bn. 1795)
Ziegenhain	Black	Silver	Buff	(2 Bns.)
Rinteln	Buff	Silver	Buff	(2 Bns. 1794, 1 Bn. 1795)
Hanau	'Royal red'	Silver	White	(4 Bns. 1794, 2 Bns. 1795)

Rheinfels – No uniform details known. Disbanded 1794.

Geismer – No uniform details known. In 1800 became 2nd Bn. of Land-Regiment Cassel, whose original 2nd Bn. had been converted to a Grenadier-Bn.

The Grenadier Battalions

Each was composed of the four grenadier companies of two infantry regiments; all were disbanded on 1 October 1795. They were often referred to by their commanders' names, and these are shown as well as their numbers:

Gren.-Bn.	*Contributing regts.*	*Commander*
1792, Nr. 1	Garde, Garde-Grenadiere	Obst. Prinz Carl von Hessen-Phillipsthal (k.i.a. Frankfurt, 2 Dec. 1792
1793, Nr. 1; 1794, Nr. 2	Erbprinz, von Kospoth	Obstlt. von Eschwege
1792, Nr. 2	Leib-Regt., Erbprinz	Obstlt. von Eschwege
1793, Nr. 2; 1794, Nr. 1	Garde-Grenadiere, Leib-Regt.	Obstlt. von Dincklage, Obstlt. von German, Major Lelong
1792–95, Nr. 3	Prinz Karl, von Lossberg	Obstlt. von Wurmb, Major Reuting
1792–93, Nr. 4	von Kospoth, von Hanstein	Obst. von Stein

Cavalry – General Notes

The bicorn, larger than that of the infantry, bore a black cockade, button-colour loop and button, crimson-within-white tassels or pompons in the corners, and plumes usually according to rank:

Hessen-Kassel Garde-Husaren, 1815 – after Steinmühler. From left to right, an officer, NCO and trooper. Black bearskins with white cords and white-and-crimson plumes. Dark blue dolman, pelisse, and shabraques; white lace, silver buttons; red cuffs, collars, and lining of officer's pelisse; black fur. Belts and harness are black with white-metal fittings. The officer's sabretasche is red and silver, his shabraque edging silver. The NCO's sabretasche is red and white with the princely cypher, his shabraque edging red.

offs., white, crimson base; NCOs, white, red tip; ORs, white, red base; trumpeters, white, red tip and base.

Hussars carried sabres and used light wooden 'Bock' saddles; other regiments used 'English' saddles and straight, basket-hilted swords. Shabraques were square, of facing colour trimmed with regimental lace (also worn by trumpeters), except for the hussars, who used long-tailed Hungarian shabraques.

The Garde du Corps, Gensd'armes and Karabiniers were all Kürassier regiments, and wore single-breasted Kollett tunics hooked closed at the front, without visible buttons. The dragoons wore long-tailed, double-breasted light blue coats, and the hussars their traditional costume.

Regimental Distinctions, 1792

Garde de Corps

Buff Kollett, crimson CLR and Swedish C; buff TB; silver BTN and lace. Scalloped silver HL; plume white, red base, for all except trumpeters – red tip and base. Steel cuirass, with crimson and silver 'cuff' for offs.; white B and gauntlets. Saddle furniture crimson for offs., red for ORs; round portmanteau; silver lace trim; eight-point Guard stars in rear corners shabraque and on holster covers; black harness, steel fittings.

Gensd'armes

White Kollett, B; poppy red CLR, C; gold BTN; gold lace for offs. and senior NCOs, red with yellow edging for ORs. Plain bicorns, plumes as Garde du Corps. Cuirass black with red cuff for ORs; offs. had crimson and silver cuff, gilt rim and rivets, gold crowned cypher at throat. Brass shoulder scales. Red saddle furniture, gold lace, coloured Hessian lion crests; black harness, brass fittings.

Karabiniers

As Gensd'armes except: light blue CLR, C, saddle furniture. Silver BTN; silver lace for offs. and senior NCOs, light blue lace edged white for ORs, and saddle furniture edging. Red cuff on offs.' cuirass. Shabraque corner/holster cover badges were Hessian crest.

Leib-Dragoner-Regiment

Plain bicorn. Poppy red F; gold lace for offs. and

Hessen-Kassel Leib-Dragoner-Regiment, 1815 – after Steinmühler. From left to right, an officer, NCO and troopers. The plumes, cockades and pompons are shown as white and crimson, the cords silver for the officer and white for the other ranks; the chinscales are gold. The light blue tunics have red collars, red shoulder straps, and for the officer red-and-gold Prussian-style epaulettes; buttons are gold, half-ball. Breeches are white for the officer, light blue with red piping for other ranks. Shabraques are light blue with silver edging for the officer, red for the other ranks: in the rear corners the princely cypher appears in silver or white. Harness is black with white metal fittings.

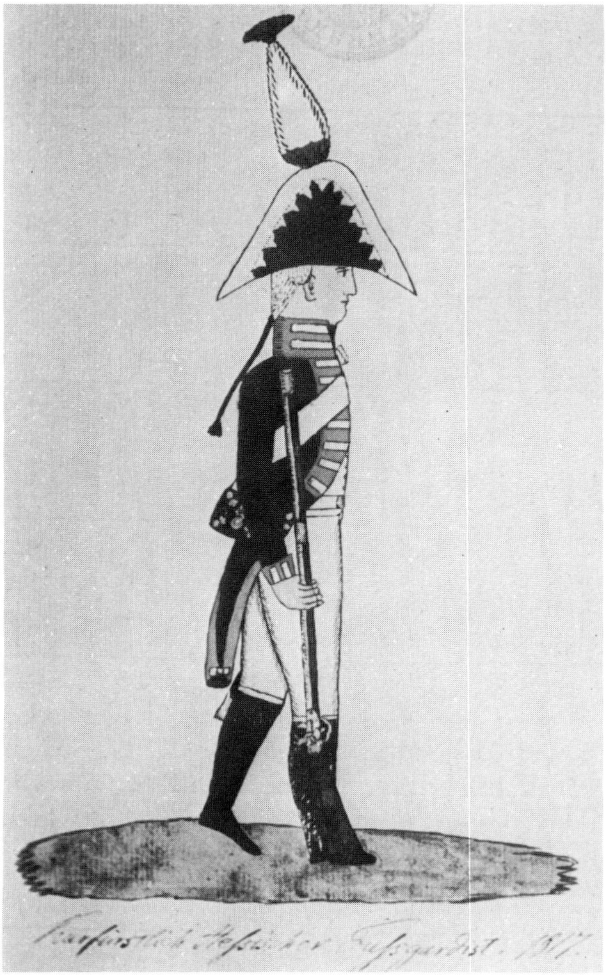

Charming naive study of a private of the Hessen-Kassel Foot Guards, 1817 – of interest since it is near-contemporary. White-and-crimson plume and white hat lace; dark blue coat with red facings, white lace, silver buttons. Musket furniture, pouch badges and belt plate are brass. Points of contention are the long coat tails – those of other ranks were much shorter than officers' – and the white 'knee cuffs' showing above the black gaiters. (Otto Helms Collection)

senior NCOs, no lace for ORs; gold BTN. White W, B. Red saddle furniture, edged gold for offs., laced crimson with yellow edging for ORs. Round red portmanteau, light blue capes, black harness with red fittings.

Prinz Friedrich Dragoner

As Leib-Dragoner except: deep yellow F and saddle furniture, silver BTN, silver lace for offs. and senior NCOs, no lace for ORs, silver/white edging to saddle furniture.

Husaren-Regiment

Black fur busby; white plume, red base; yellow bag. Yellow dolman, light blue pelisse; light blue CLR, C; black fur trim; silver/white lace, BTN. White B, yellow Charivari; yellow boots for offs., black for ORs. Light blue saddle furniture with silver/yellow scalloped lace according to rank, and crowned cypher. Black Hungarian harness, white fittings. Moustaches except for trumpeters.

Uniforms of the Kur-Hessischen Legion, 1809

See commentary on Plate G3.

Infantry:

Garde-Grenadier-Bataillon

Black Austrian grenadier bearskins; white grenade badge on front above black peak edged silver; red bag, white piping, white cords and tassel to right side; white-over-red plume on left. Dark blue coat without shoulder straps; red CLR, Swedish C, L, TB; white W, B, belts; silver BTN; high black gaiters; rank badges as 1806.

Leichtes Infanterie-Bataillon

Austrian shako, black peak and chinstrap, large frontal red-within-white cockade below red-within-white pompon linked by silver loop and BTN. Offs. had falling black horsehair plumes; ORs, black plume with red tip and base; NCOs, red base only. Dark green, single-breasted tunics; eight silver BTN; red CLR, Swedish C, TB. Dark green B; hussar boots; black belts, silver fittings. Offs. wore silver contre-epaulette and aiguillette on right shoulder, wide silver waist sash, silver thigh knots, white gauntlets, silver boot trim, silver-hilted sabre in steel sheath on black slings. The Regiments Kürfurst and von Biesenrodt appear in the Legion's records, but never mustered more than a handful of men.

Cavalry:

Leib-Dragoner-Eskadron

Austrian heavy-cavalry pattern helmet, black leather with brass fittings, crowned 'WK' cypher on front plate, red-over-white crest, brass chin-scales. Light blue double-breasted tunic with field poppy red CLR, Swedish C, TB edging; light blue TB, shoulder straps; silver BTN. Buff gauntlets; grey overalls with silver BTN and black leather booting. White belts; Austrian heavy cavalry sword; white sheepskin saddle cover edged red; light blue holster covers edged red; black harness, silver fittings.

Husaren-Eskadron

Infantry shako, red-and-white cords, white-over-

red plume. Pale yellow dolman, light blue CLR, C; silver BTN, white lace. Light blue pelisse, black fur trim. Red-and-white sash. Grey overalls, silver BTN, black booting. Black bandolier and slings; light blue sabretasche with white crowned 'WK', white edging. Steel-furnished Austrian hussar sabre. Harness as dragoons but black sheepskin, edged light blue. Hair was worn queued and with side-locks, and moustaches were worn.
Artillery Detachment Infantry uniform, dark blue with crimson F, gold BTN.

Hessen-Kassel Uniforms, from 1813

Once again the Prussians served as the Kürfurst's model when he ordered uniforms designed for his restored army in 1813. The exceptional detail was the anachronistic pigtail, an eccentricity which Wilhelm I re-introduced not – as many sources suppose – immediately in 1813, but as late as 1816. The theoretical uniform details are listed here: it goes without saying that for many months these ambitious and punctilious patterns existed only in the minds of the designers, and in practice the men wore a mixture of outdated uniforms, civilian clothes and rags.
Guard Infantry
Prussian-style leather-reinforced shakos; white cords for ORs, silver-and-red cords for offs.; silver chinscales; red-within-white pompon; plumes white with red tip for ORs, white with red tip and base for NCOs, white with red base for offs.; small Hessian lion badges in BTN colour each side of shako for offs., replacing Prussian eagles. Two loops Prussian-style Guard lace on CLR and Swedish C, silver. Double-breasted coat worn with lapels buttoned over. Senior NCOs had silver edging on C, or C and CLR. Offs. had red-and-silver sash and portepee. Belts, B, white. Black half-gaiters, black buttons; offs. wore short boots, straight at top. Eight-point silver star on pouch. French muskets, sabres. Drummers wore dark blue swallows' nests with red-and-silver lace; brass drums had red-and-blue striped hoops.
Distinctions:
Schweizer Leibgarde
Light blue coat; field poppy red CLR, C, TB, shoulder straps; silver lace, BTN, right-hand aiguillette.
Leib-Grenadier-Garde
Black bearskin, silver plate with 'WK' under electoral cap; white cords, plumes of rank. Dark blue coat, field poppy red CLR, C, TB, shoulder straps; silver BTN, lace.
Garde-Grenadier-Regiment, or 'Regiment-Garde'
All detail as for Leib-Grenadier-Garde except only the two grenadier companies wore bearskins, the musketeer battalions wearing a shako with silver grenade badge.
Line Infantry
Each regiment eventually consisted of two grenadier companies, detached from the parent regiments and serving in four-company grenadier battalions; two musketeer battalions and a fusilier battalion, each of four companies. Fusiliers were supposed to receive black belts, but these were delayed. Facings were shown at CLR, C, shoulder straps; TB supposedly red throughout, but report by Gen. Maj. von Gaudi, 29.4.14 suggests at least 'Kürfurst' had yellow TB at that date. No lace, BTN, on CLR or C; dark blue CF, three BTN.
Distinctions:
Regiment Kürfurst Lemon yellow F, gold BTN
Regiment Kürprinz White F, gold BTN
Regiment Landgraf Karl Red F, gold BTN
Regiment 'vacant von Wurmb' Crimson F, silver BTN *(from 2.1.14, von Solms)*

The Grenadier-Bataillon von Haller was

Hessen-Darmstadt officer's gorget, 1815; silver with gold lion and wreath. After an example in Darmstadt Castle Museum.

formed from the grenadiers of the first two regiments, the Grenadier-Bataillon von Schmidt from the second two.

Jäger-Bataillon

As line infantry but dark green coat, red F (Swedish C), crimson TB, silver BTN, no lace. Grey B; rifles; black belts.

Foot Artillery

Two and a half batteries. Line infantry style uniform, dark blue coat (Swedish C); crimson F, yellow-laced CLR, gold BTN. Brass grenade, crossed cannons badge on shako and pouch. White B; black belts.

Horse Artillery

Half battery. As Foot Artillery, but short, straight-topped boots with screw-in steel spurs; light cavalry sabres in steel sheaths.

Cavalry Uniforms, 1814

Garde du Corps

One squadron. Bavarian Raupenhelm in black leather, silver plate and front band with 'WK' below electoral cap, over 'GARDE DU CORPS'; black crest – stuffed wool for ORs and corporals, bearskin for offs. and senior NCOs; black chinstraps edged with silver chains, later perhaps silver chinscales; plume, according to rank, at left.

Buff tunic, field poppy red CLR, TB edging, Swedish C; buff TB; silver lace loops on CLR, C; silver BTN. White B, heavy cuffed boots, buckled spurs for parades; for other duties, grey overalls, silver BTN, red piping, short boots with screw-in spurs. Offs. wore red leather bandoliers with silver lace, and silver-and-red waist sashes tasselled at left. ORs wore white crossed bandoliers. Brass-hilted heavy cavalry swords, steel sheaths, white slings. Saddle furniture red, edged double white (silver for offs.) lace, with eight-point star in corners. Black heavy-cavalry harness, steel fittings. On some occasions steel cuirasses were worn, with brass shoulder scales, brass rivets, a red cuff edged white and a white waist belt. Those of offs. had a gilt eight-point star motif high on the breast.

Trumpeters had red helmet crests and red swallows' nests laced with silver; silver trumpets were fitted with red-and-silver cords.

Garde-Husaren

One squadron. Black fur busby, red bag, white cords, plume according to rank. Dark blue dolman, five rows silver BTN, silver lace, field poppy red CLR, C. Dark blue pelisse, silver BTN and lace, black fur trim. White B, red-and-silver barrel sash, black belts and bandoliers; red sabretasche, white edging and 'WK' beneath electoral cap for ORs, silver lace and crowned Hessian lion amid trophies for offs.; silver buckles. Hussar boots, silver lace and tassel for offs.; sabres with gilt hilts, brass sheaths. Dark blue shabraque, silver-and-red edging. Black Polish-style harness, silver fittings; heavy decoration of white shells for offs.

Line Cavalry

Leib-Dragoner-Regiment

Four squadrons. Shako, red-within-white cockade and pompon, plume according to rank; white cords (silver-and-red for offs. and senior NCOs); silver peak edging, chinscales. Light blue double-breasted tunic; field poppy red CLR, Swedish C, shoulder straps; light blue TB edged poppy red; silver BTN. White or buff leather B, white belts, straight-topped boots with screw-in steel spurs for parades; otherwise grey overalls, silver BTN, red piping. Offs. wore white gauntlets. Brass-hilted sabres, steel sheaths. Light blue shabraque

Hessen-Kassel infantry drum, *c.*1785. The body is brass, the hoops red and white; note the princely crest. (Schloss Friedrichstein Museum)

Hessen-Kassel infantry Leibfahne, *c.* 1790. This reconstruction by the author is based on remnants of an actual example preserved in Schloss Friedrichstein, but the colours are so faded as to be scarcely recognisable. The field is white silk, the embroidery apparently gold, with coloured central crest as follows, clockwise from 1 o'clock: six-point silver star on black field over gold field; two gold rampant lions on red field; silver nails and nettle leaves on red field round a red-over-silver shield; red and gold bars and heraldic ordinaries around a gold-over-red shield; two eight-point silver stars on a black field over a gold field; red rampant lion with blue crown on red field; red cross of Lorraine on silver field. The central crest is the red-and-white striped Hessian lion on a blue field. The princely cypher 'WL' appears in the corner medallions and on the finial.

and round portmanteau edged red for ORs, silver with red outer edge for offs.; in rear corner 'WK' under electoral cap, all white. Black light-cavalry harness, steel fittings. Trumpeters' plumes red, swallows' nests red edged silver, brass trumpets with red-and-white cords.

Husaren-Regiment

Four squadrons. Shakos as Leib-Dragoner, remainder as Garde-Husaren.

Landwehr Infantry

Gen.Maj. von Gaudi's notes give following description:

'Each infantry and cavalry regiment will raise a Freiwillige Jäger detachment of 200 men after the Prussian example. In each of the provinces Niederhessen, Oberhessen and Fürstenthum Hanau two Landwehr battalions will be raised.' (24.11.13)

These Landwehr wore simple shakos in black oilcloth covers with the Landwehr cross in white on the front; dark blue Litewka double-breasted coats with full skirts and silver buttons; grey trousers and black belts. Facings were shown on the collar and Polish cuffs: 1 Regt., crimson; 2nd, black; 3rd, red. (Another source, I. R. Worringer, *Zeitschrift für Heereskünde Nrs. 40, 41, 42* in April 1932, gives the sequence as red, black and crimson.)

Hessen-Kassel Campaign Summary

1793–95 Low Countries, Lorraine, Champagne, Westfalia, Upper Rhine

1793 Expedition to the Isle of Wight (Gensd'armes, inf. regts. 'von Linsingen, Prinz Karl only)

1809 Campaign in Saxony (Kur-Hessisches Legion only)

1814–15 Upper Rhine and France

Colours and Standards

Practically no written data has been found concerning the colours and standards of this army in 1792–1806. It is known that in the American War of Independence each company carried its own colour; it is not known how many regimental colours were carried within each battalion. Many examples were described by Gherardi Davis in his *Regimental Colours of the Revolution*, New York, 1907; unfortunately he erroneously classed some as being Leib or sovereign's colours, but as all are non-white this cannot be so.

In the new museum in Schloss Friedrichstein at Bad Wildungen near Kassel there is exhibited the remains of a Hessen-Kassel Leibfahne. Of white silk, it bears in the centre the great crest of the Landgraf, held by golden lions, under a Landgraf's crown and other trophies of arms. In each corner the crowned cypher 'WL' dates it directly to our period. The gilt finial of the white pike – a convincing detail – bore a lion with crown and sword.

Regimental colours were painted on silk, with, in the centre, the red-and-white striped Hessian lion with crown and sword on a light blue field within gold laurel wreaths tied with pink ribbon and under a Landgraf's crown. The crown rested on a pale pink scroll bearing 'NESCIT PERICULA' in gold. Small gold corner wreaths enclosed a gold 'WL'; in the centre of each side was a silver flaming grenade. The gilt finial bore the cypher, and the staff colour varied with the regiment. All colours were decorated with silver-and-crimson cords and tassels. Thalmann's excellent work in the Marburg Archives gives a series of regimental colours, all dating from 1786, in detail, and smaller and much less distinct portrayals of white Leibfahnen. Some colours were of solid colour, others had 'flaming' diagonal crosses in a contrasting colour. Thalmann shows:

Regiment Garde . . . All white
Garde-Grenadier-Regt. . . . All red
Erbprinz . . . Red, light blue cross
Prinz Karl . . . All dark green
Leib-Regt. . . . Yellow, red cross
von Kospoth . . . Black, buff cross
von Lossberg . . . Orange, light green cross
von Heymel . . . All yellow

Light troops and artillery carried no colours.

Cavalry Standards

Thalmann, and exhibits in Schloss Friedrichstein, are the only sources found. Thalmann gives the following overview. Each squadron would seem to have carried a standard (hussars carried none). The Leib-Eskadron carried a white Leib-Estandarte, the others each having a coloured standard. No details of the relationship between squadron and colour are known. Examples are:

Garde du Corps . . . All white, in vexillum form, suspended on silver chains from a staff with solid silver Hessian lion finial; embroidered overall
Gensd'armes . . . Red
Karabiniers . . . Red

Leib-Dragoner . . . Red
Prinze Friedrich Dragoner . . . Yellow

All were square, and bore in the centre the embroidered rampant Hessian lion striped in silver and white; fringes were of button-colour. The corners of the standards of the Gensd'armes and Leib-Dragoner bore silver cyphers (in 1786, 'FL'); those of the other line regiments are shown blank. Pikes were red, finials gilt spearheads; cords of silver and crimson, with tassels, hung about two-thirds of the way down the standards.

Infantry Colours, 1814

New colours were presented to all existing regiments at the Martinskirche in Kassel on 1 March 1814. The design had altered radically since the period 1792–1806. Although no surviving written evidence has been discovered, existing colours at

Hessen-Darmstadt infantry, 1799. This Knötel plate shows the men without pouches in order to display the lapel details clearly. Left to right: 1st Leib-Btl. (crimson facings, silver buttons); 2nd Leib-Btl. (orange facings, silver buttons); Leib-Regt. (red facings, silver buttons); Regt. Landgraf (white facings, gold buttons); Regt. Erbprinz (pink facings, silver buttons); Depot-Btl. (dull yellow facings, gold buttons); Land-Regt. (light blue facings, gold buttons); officer of Regt. Erbprinz – note sash worn over coat, a style adopted in Prussia somewhat later. With the exception of the Depot-Btl. all regiments had dark blue rectangular cuff flaps decorated with three lace loops; those of the Depot-Btl. were plain. (By kind permission W. Spemann Verlag, Franck'sche Verlagshandlung, Stuttgart)

Schloss Friedrichstein give the following picture:

Each regiment had (at least) two colours, a white Leibfahne and one or more crimson Regimentsfahnen. The Leibfahne was square. On the obverse it bore centrally a red-and-white striped Hessian lion with sword on a light blue shield, below a light blue scroll bearing 'MIT GOTT

FÜR FÜRST UND VATERLAND'; around the shield, golden oak and laurel branches, in each corner golden sunrays. The reverse was the same except that the central device was the golden cypher 'WK' under an electoral cap. The pike was 3.15m long, light blue, with a pierced brass tip bearing the cypher under the cap. The silk was nailed to the pike with dome-headed gilt nails.

The crimson regimental colours were the same as the Leibfahne except that the scroll bore 'GOTT SCHUTZT DEN DER AUF IHN BAUT' (God Protects Those Who Build On Him') on the colour/s of the Regt. Prinz von Solms-Braunfels, and 'MEINEN TREUEN HESSEN' on that of the Regt. Kürprinz. No data has been found to suggest that cavalry standards were presented in 1813–15.

Hessen-Kassel Ordinärfahne, Regiment Prinz von Solms, 1814. Crimson field; gold finial, nails and corner rays; light blue shield and pike; red-and-white lion, white scroll, black inscription. From an example in the Schloss Friedrichstein Museum.

The Plates

A: Hessen-Darmstadt: Officer, Chevaulegers, 1790–1803

This regiment was eventually destroyed in a desperate rearguard action at the Beresina crossing in Russia in 1812. The figure, from a plate in the regimental history, shows an officer in full dress. The British influence is plain; the peculiar helmet, and the chevron decoration on the coat sleeves and tails, both approximate to late 18th-century British light cavalry styles. The black leather helmet had a skull of truncated conical shape behind the curved front shield; the black crest extended in an arc from the back of the skull to the top of the front shield. The elaborate parade harness is decorated with hundreds of cowrie shells.

B1: Hessen-Darmstadt: Private, 3rd Company, Leichtes Infanterie-Bataillon, 1790

After a plate in the regimental history. The

traditional sombre colours accord with the rôle of this unit, which recruited small, agile men. The hair is still worn queued, curled and powdered, a time-consuming and horribly unhygeinic practice. The blue hat pompon and sabre tassel identify the company. He carries on the left hip the calfskin pack and grey canvas haversack which indicate summer field service marching order. The weapon is a smoothbore musket – only a proportion of the unit carried rifles; note red sling.

B2: Hessen-Darmstadt: Oberst, Artillery, 1792
From a plate in the regimental history. The Hessen-Darmstadt artillery were the only gunners of the Grande Armée to bring their cannon back from the Russian disaster of 1812. Black facings were adopted by many continental artillery corps; they had certain practical advantages in the days of black powder, when fighting the guns was an extremely dirty job. As a mounted officer this colonel wears jacked boots and buckled spurs. His gold-tipped cane with silver tasselled cord is a sign of office, but the important indication of officer status was the silver-and-red portepee on the sword hilt.

B3: Hessen-Darmstadt: Hornist, Füsilier-Bataillon, Brigade Landgraf, June 1803
After a plate in the regimental history. The Prussian influence was strong in the armies of many German states; elderly men could still remember Frederick the Great, and by a process of 'sympathetic magic' it seems to have been hoped that by copying Prussian uniforms and drill they could inherit his prowess. The small, two-flap bicorn worn by B2 and B3 is copied from the Prussian infantry of the 1780s. The horn is of typical German design; its carrying note was used to pass signals when fighting in extended order. Drummers, hornists and musicians wore the 'swallows' nest' shoulder wing in facing colour, decorated with button-colour lace.

C1: Hessen-Darmstadt: Officer, Leib-Regiment, 1807–09
After Knötel, and a plate in the regimental history. After about 1808 the coat was worn

Hessen-Kassel, Leib-Grenadier-Garde and Regiment Garde, 1814. A sketch by Knötel in the regimental history. The Prussian style of coat may be seen here, with its collar lace; the two rows of silver buttons were spaced narrowly on the chest. The grenadier's black bearskin is of Austrian pattern with red backing, and a silver plate bearing a rampant lion holding the 'Guards star'. Collar and cuff lace, shoulder straps and belts are white, the musket and equipment apparently French. The private of the Regt. Garde is dressed as the grenadier except for his (French?) shako with white-metal badge and chinscales, white cords and white-and-red cockade.

closed to the waist with the sash over it. By this time the hated pigtail had disappeared from most European armies, although Hessen-Kassel retained it from 1816 to about 1821. There are several descriptions of the plume adopted by the Hessians in 1806 after confusion with Prussians at Jena. Some say red, others red with a black tip, others black, or black with a red tip. No final answer has been found, but red with a black base for officers and a black tip for NCOs seems likely.

C2: Hessen-Darmstadt: Trooper, Garde du Corps, 1809
This palace bodyguard did not comply with the

change in plume colours. Note also that although the sabretasche bears the new cypher of Grand Duke Ludwig I, the sword hilt still carries the old 'LLX' cypher. Members of this élite unit were drawn from the aristocracy, and ranked as officers even though nominally titled trooper or sergeant. After a plate in the regimental history.

C3: Hessen-Darmstadt: Sergeant, Foot Artillery, 1809
After a plate in the regimental history. This unit was part of the Hessian force which fought at Aspern-Essling in 1809. The coat was of the pattern worn by all dismounted units apart from the Regt. Gross- und Erbprinz. Two loops decorated the red-piped horizontal false pockets. French rank badges had been adopted in 1806, but the contre-epaulettes were peculiar to this state. They were edged in the facing colour for privates, and silver for NCOs. Note that the gaiter buttons are brass even though those on the coat are tin. The confusion over the plumes worn by the Hessians is reflected here. Four horizontal grenades decorated the turn-backs.

D1: Hessen-Darmstadt: Corporal, Grenadier Company, Regt. Gross- und Erbprinz; Spain, 1809
After Knötel. As a member of the Confederation of the Rhine the state was required to make a military contribution to Napoleon's war effort: this regiment was Hesse's contribution to the Peninsular War. Re-organised and re-badged in the French manner, it saw much heavy fighting before passing into British captivity at Badajoz in 1812. The uniform shown here was probably the exception rather than the rule; resupply of clothing was very infrequent, and the regimental history records that coat tails were cut off to make patches for the rest of the outfit. The French equipment and armament replaced the old and varied designs carried before the regiment entered French service.

D2: Hessen-Darmstadt: Officer, Leib-Regiment, 1812
After various sources. The Hessians provided six battalions of infantry, a regiment of horse and the associated artillery batteries (eight guns) for Napoleon's Russian adventure of 1812. They served in the 4th Division, I Corps and the 34th Division, XI Corps (infantry), and the 30th Light Cavalry Brigade, IX Corps (Chevaulegers).

Hessen-Kassel, Swiss Life Guards, 1815. At left is a private in full dress – red and blue plumes, red and blue cockade, gold button; blue tunic and breeches with red stripes edged in white; silver and red baldric; silver, red and blue tassels to halberd; red stockings; red and blue shoe-knots. In the centre is an NCO in service dress – white-over-red plume; dark blue coat with red facings, silver lace and buttons; white breeches and gauntlets; white-and-red sword knot; brown cane with gilt knob. At right is an officer in service dress – as for the NCO except for a silver hat-brooch, silver portepee, and spurred boots. (After Steinmühler)

The sash had now been abandoned in favour of the silver gorget as a sign of office when on duty. The cut of the coat had changed in that the lapels were now cut straight across the bottom at waist level, and no waistcoat was shown.

D3: Hessen-Darmstadt: Trooper, Garde-Chevaulegers, 1812

After Knötel. The British light dragoon-style helmet had been replaced in about 1806 by the high, domed type shown here, probably copied from the Bavarians, although the chevrons on sleeves and tails were retained (see MAA 106, *Napoleon's German Allies (4): Bavaria*). It is not known how the French rank badges were incorporated into this sleeve decoration. Dark green overalls with red stripes cover the white parade breeches. Wiped out on the Beresina on 27 November 1812, the regiment was re-raised in 1813. A narrow bandolier supported a small black pouch at the back, partly hidden by the carbine belt; from the latter a small strap connected with a ramrod fixed along the top of the pouch.

E1: Hessen-Darmstadt: Officer, 1st Company, Freiwillige Jäger, 1813–14

After Knötel. As in most other German states, Hessen-Darmstadt raised volunteer companies in addition to conscripted line troops to fight Napoleon in the 'wars of liberation' of 1813–15. Volunteers paid for their own uniforms and equipment, and were given better treatment than conscripts. They were concentrated into élite companies attached to conscript battalions for scouting and skirmishing duties – hence the Jäger uniform and the rifles they carried. Their civilian jobs were kept open for them during their service, and it was promised that their later careers would benefit for their having served the Fatherland. While on campaign they wore an oak sprig (or fir, in winter) on the shako – a common practice in Austria, Prussia, and many other German states.

E2: Hessen-Darmstadt: Officer, Leib-Garde-Regiment, 1814

After a plate in Darmstadt Archives. Hidden here are three-point red-piped horizontal coat pockets. On parades officers now wore black plumes with a red base inserted into a silver pompon with a red horizontal ring. NCOs had black plumes with a red tip, and red pompons with a silver ring. Privates' plain black plumes were worn from a pompon in company colour (see text) and surmounted by either a red tuft or a red pompon – sources differ. While on duty the silver gorget was still worn, and the French ranking was retained. In winter and on field service the white breeches were replaced by blue trousers worn over the boots.

E3: Hessen-Darmstadt: Private, Regiment Prinz Emil, 1814

Newly raised in 1813–14, this regiment was obviously clothed, armed and equipped with the then-available French-pattern items. French rank badges were still worn, but the peculiar Hessian contre-epaulettes were replaced in 1814 by dark blue shoulder straps edged at the sides and rounded end in regimental facing colour. The white-and-yellow pompon indicates the 5th Company. After Knötel – who omits the lapel laces, which were perhaps introduced late in 1814. Hidden here are three-point pink-piped horizontal coat pockets.

F1: Hessen-Kassel: NCO, Füsiliers, Leib-Regiment, 1792

The headdress of the fusilier companies within Hessen-Kassel infantry regiments resembled the grenadier's traditional mitre, but the frontal plate was rather lower, and the crown of the headpiece rose to a point and was tipped with a metal spike in button colour. The cloth of the crown was usually in facing colour. The metal headband was decorated with grenades and trophies; the design of band and plate differed with each regiment. This NCO in parade dress carries a halberd; these, and officers' spontoons, were discarded for all except parade duty at about this period, and by 1803 they had vanished altogether. NCO status is indicated by the silver lace, the cane, the red-and-white sabre strap, the gauntlets, and the absence of musket and pouch. After Müller and Carl.

F2: Hessen-Kassel: Officer, Hussars, 1792

The dressy and expensive uniform, complete with the yellow boots copied from those of senior

Turkish officers, may seem hopelessly unsuited for the campaign tasks of light cavalry scouting units even in an age of conspicuous military glamour. In fact, in this as in many other small German states, the hussars were more a gendarmerie in peacetime than a battlefield force. They were distributed over the whole country, patrolling country roads and borders in small groups of three or four men, and chasing deserters – of whom there were many! This was excellent training for their tactical rôle in wartime. After Müller and Carl.

F3: Hessen-Kassel: Drummer, Regiment Garde, 1792
From contemporary plates in the Darmstadt archives it appears that most infantry regiments employed Negro boys as drummers. The stylised turban is shown only vaguely in the original source, as is the exact pattern of the lace; but it seems that the red figures are miniature crowned cyphers – 'WL' for 'Wilhelm, Landgraf'. Each regiment had its own distinctive lace, and the Garde were the dandies of this small army. The waistcoat and breeches are yellow. After Müller and Carl.

G1: Hessen-Kassel: Officer, Light Infantry, Kur-Hessian Legion, 1809
In the wake of Austria's brave but foolhardy attempt to overthrow Napoleon in 1809 several Free Corps were raised in Bohemia, among them the 'Black Brunswickers' and the Kur-Hessians. The latter, although disbanded after a few months, did see action in a spirited thrust into southern Germany which caused much trouble for Jerome Bonaparte, then attempting to secure his position as king of Westfalia. Almost all items of uniform and equipment were of Austrian design or origin. The hair is unpowdered but queued. After a contemporary plate by Hass in the Kassel Archives.

G2: Hessen-Kassel: Trumpeter, Karabiniers, 1792
Apart from the shoulder and sleeve decorations, trumpeters were also distinguished by their crimson plume tips and bases. This regiment had in fact abandoned the wearing of cuirasses a few years previously, but the cut of the tunic still reflected their original armoured rôle, being of buff leather without front buttons. The leather breeches were normally whitened for parades. Troopers wore moustaches, but officers and trumpeters were clean-shaven. After Müller and Carl.

G3: Hessen-Kassel: Officer of Grenadiers, Garde-Grenadiere, 1792
The fur on the Austrian bearskin was set pointing upwards at the front and downwards at the back and sides. The large 18th-century style of gorget was still worn. The officers' musket, with red leather sling, was of fine workmanship, and had the sovereign's cypher engraved on the blade of the bayonet. The lid of the silver cartouche worn frontally on the waist belt is decorated with a gilt cypher and trophies of arms. After Mühler and Carl.

H1: Hessen-Kassel: Officer, Regiment Landgraf Karl, 1814
While officers, whose appearance depended upon private means, probably blossomed into the colours of the restored Electorate fairly soon after Hessen-Kassel's liberation, it would have been many months before any substantial numbers of troops could have been fitted out with the prescribed new uniforms. Prussian influence was again noticeable in the design of the uniform; note the small gilt lions at the sides of the shako, in the position occupied by small eagles on the shakos of Prussian officers. Officers wore no epaulettes, however, but carried malacca canes instead. Senior NCOs had their plumes tipped and based with red, and wore silver sabre-strap tassels; gold lacing edged the top and front of their collars, and the top of their cuffs. Junior NCOs had gold-laced collars only. After a plate by Steinmühler (who was a Premierlieutenant in the Garde-Grenadiere) but with altered hairstyle.

H2: Hessen-Kassel: NCO of Jägers, 1814
The newly-raised Jäger-Bataillon had crimson facings, and Steinmühler shows silver buttons and lace, the officers' shakos bearing silver chains and lions; other ranks' shakos were decorated only with the red-and-white cockade. The straight sword-bayonet or Hirschfänger had an antler-horn hilt. Privates' plumes were plain dark green,

officers' red-tipped. Once again, we have 'sent this man for a haircut' – Steinmühler shows an anachronistic pigtail, which was not in fact re-introduced for another two years.

H3: Hessen-Kassel: NCO, Horse Artillery, 1816
This corps wore black plumes, with the usual red rank distinctions. Leatherwork was black, the pouch flap bearing brass crossed cannons under a grenade. Officers' shako cords were silver, however, despite the button and lace colour being gold. The plain round cuffs bore two lace buttonhole loops in gold or yellow according to rank. NCOs of Foot Artillery followed infantry practice – gold-laced collars and cuffs – but in the mounted branch the distinction was the replacement of yellow loops with gold on collar and cuff. The shako is the Russian 'Kiwer', but some personnel are known to have worn a Prussian pattern. The pigtail of 1816–*c.*1822 is shown here. After Steinmühler.

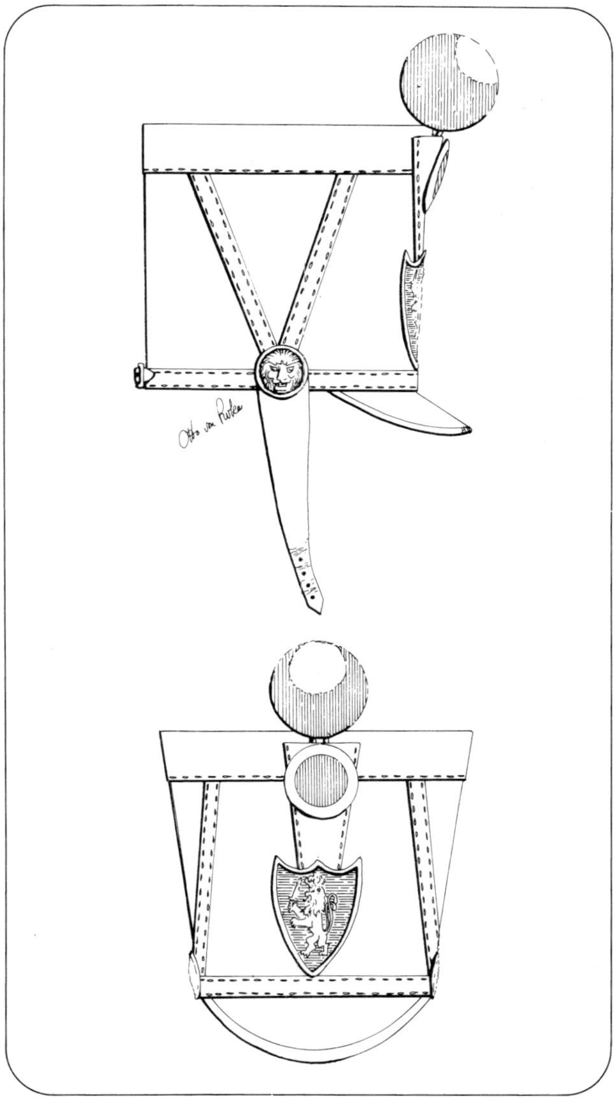

Hessen-Darmstadt infantry shako of French pattern, 1809–15; white-within-red pompon, red-within-white cockade, white metal shield and chinstrap boss. After a surviving example in Darmstadt Castle Museum.

Sources:

Hessen-Darmstadt

Bauer von Bauer, *Geschichte der Grossherzoglich Hessischen Garde-Unteroffiziers-Compagnie*, Darmstadt, 1898

Beck, Fritz, *Geschichte der Grossherzoglichen Hessischen Fahnen und Standarten*, Berlin, 1895

Beck, Fritz, *Geschichte des 1. Grossherzoglich Hessischen Infanterie- (Leibgarde-) Regiments Nr. 115*, Berlin, 1899

Beck, Fritz, *Geschichte des Infanterie-Regiments Kaiser Wilhelm (2. Grossherzoglich Hessisches) Nr. 116*, Berlin

Beck, Fritz, *Geschichte des Grossherzoglich Hessischen Gendarmerie-Korps 1763–1905*, Darmstadt, 1905

Beck, Fritz, *Geschichte des 1. Grossherzoglich Hessischen Dragoner-Regiments (Garde-Dragoner-Regiments) Nr. 25*, Darmstadt, 1878

Keim, A., *Geschichte des Infanterie-Leibregiments Grossherzogin (3. Grossherzoglich Hessisches) Nr. 117*, Berlin, 1903

Keim, A., *Geschichte des 4. Grossherzoglich Hessischen Infanterie-Regiments (Prinz Karl) Nr. 118*, Berlin, 1879

Hessen-Kassel

'Stamm- und Rangliste von Hochfürstlich Hessischen Corps' for the years 1794–1806, Kassel, 1856

Losch, Philipp, *Die Kurhessischen Regimenter*, Melsungen, 1900

Carl, J. H., & Müller, J. C., *Hochfürstl. Hessen-Casselis. Saemtlichen Trouppen*, Darmstadt; a series of colour plates painted in about 1788.

Thalmann, G. F., *Abbildung und Beschreibung des Fürstes Hessen-Casselschen Militair-Stantes under der Regierung Landgraf Friedrich des Zweiten bis zum Jahr 1786*; a collection of over 100 contemporary watercolours.

Davis, G., *Regimental Colours in the Revolution*, New York, 1907; a limited edition of 125 copies von Steinmüller, *Kurhessischen Uniformbilder 1814*; a series of contemporary watercolours.

Kossechi, Carl von, *Geschichte des Königlich Preussischen 2. Hessischen Husaren-Regiments Nr. 14*, Leipzig, 1887

Dechend, *Geschichte des Füsilier-Regiments von Gersdorff (Hessisches) Nr. 80*, Berlin, 1901

Has, Dr. W., *Geschichte des 1. Kurhessischen Feldartillerie-Regiments Nr. 19*, Marburg, 1913

General

Knötel-Sieg, *Handbuch der Uniformenkunde*, Hamburg, 1966

Knötel, R., *Mitteilungen zur Uniformenkunde*

Weiland, C. F., *Darstellung der Stärke und Organisation der Kaiserlich Französischen Armee und Ihrer Allierten in Jahre 1807 und 1812*, Weimar, 1807 & 1812

Documents and exhibits in the following museums and collections:

Ministry of Defence Library (Army and Central), Whitehall; Sammlung Preussischer Kulturbesitz, Berlin; Wehrhistorisch- und Jagd-Museum, Schloss Friedrichstein, Bad Wildungen; Hessisches Staatsarchiv, Marburg; Hessisches Staatsarchiv, Kassel; Hessisches Staatsarchiv, Darmstadt; Murhardt-Bibliothek, Kassel; Zentral Bibliothek der Bundeswehr, Düsseldorf.

Notes sur les planches en couleur

A L'influence anglaise est visible dans ce modèle de coiffure de la cavalerie légère et dans les chevrons de la tunique.

B1 Le pompon bleu et la soutache du sabre identifient la compagnie. La chevelure est encore poudrée, frisée et en queue-de-rat. Seule une partie de cette unité avait des fusils au lieu de mousquets. **B2** La seule unité d'artillerie qui ait rapporté son canon de Russie en 1812. Officier supérieur, donc à cheval et portant des bottes hautes. La canne était réservée aux officiers. **B3** Cet uniforme montre l'influence prussienne. Les cors avaient remplacé les tambours dans les unités d'infanterie légère; des 'nids d'hirondelle' ornaient les épaules des musiciens.

C1 Plus de queue-de-rat, et la tunique est maintenant fermée à la taille. Les avis diffèrent quant à la couleur des plumes: cette combinaison est plausible. **C2** Les soldats et sous-officiers de cette unité d'élite, tous issus de l'aristocratie, assumaient un statut d'officier auprès des hommes d'autres unités. **C3** Insignes français de grades, maintenant portés par toutes les unités de la Confédération du Rhine, mais ces contre-épaulettes distinguent les troupes de Hesse-Darmstadt.

D1 Cet uniforme a subi une forte influence français. Peu de soldats étaient en fait aussi élégamment et complètement vêtus aux premières lignes en Espagne. **D2** Le gorget a remplacé l'écharpe pour indiquer le statut d'officier et la tunique était coupée horizontalement sous la taille, cachant le gilet. **D3** Le régiment, decimé au passage de la Bérézina, portait maintenant une coiffure de style bavarois au lieu du style anglais précédent.

E1 Les compagnies de ces volontaires d'élite, qui avaient l'uniforme traditionnel Jäger et des fusils, étaient détachés auprès des bataillons de recrues d'infanterie en tant qu'éclaireurs. **E2** Des pantalons bleus portés au-dessus des bottes remplaçaient les culottes de cheval blanches pendant l'hiver et en campagne. **E3** Levée en 1813–14, cette unité utilisait beaucoup d'équipement français. Les contre-épaulettes furent remplacées en 1814 par des pattes d'epaules plus conventionnelles.

F1 Les sous-officiers portaient encore des hallebardes aux parades. Les détails du calot des fusiliers variaient de régiment en régiment. **F2** Uniforme de hussard typique de l'époque, avec bottes jaunes claires originellement copiées sur les officiers turcs. **F3** La plupart des régiments d'infanterie semblent avoir eu des tambours noirs avec des tuniques richement décorées de cordonnets dont les motifs variaient d'un régiment à l'autre.

G1 Ce corps éphémère de volontaires avait un uniforme et un équipement de style autrichien. **G2** Bien que cette unité ait abandonné les cuirasses depuis un certain temps, la coupe de cette tunique trahit encore les origines de l'uniforme. Les trompettes étaient rasés, avaient des manches et des épaulez ornementées, ainsi que des plumes rouges à la base et au sommet. **G3** Forte influence autrichienne. La peu d'ours du calot avait le poil couché vers le haut sur le devant et vers le bas sur les côtés et derrière. Baionnette finement gravée avec chiffre.

H1 Forte influence prussienne dans cet uniforme. **H2** La queue-de-rat n'a pas été reprise avant 1816. Uniforme Jäger typique, y compris le 'Hirschfanger' à manche de corne. **H3** Le shako russe 'Kiwer' n'était pas unanimement porté car certaines troupes avaient le modèle prussien. Les galons sur les manchettes étaient jaunes ou or selon les grades.

Farbtafeln

A1: Der britische Einfluss ist im Entwurf des Leichtkavallerie-helmes und der Armwinkelauszeichnungen zu erkennen.

B1: Blaue Hutpommel und Säbelquaste lassen die Kompanie erkennen. Bemerke, dass das Haar noch gepudert, gelockt und in einem Zopf getragen wurde. Nur ein Teil dieser Einheit trug Stutze, also Gegenstück zur Muskete. **B2:** Die einzige Artillerieeinheit, die ihre Geschütze von Russland im Jahr 1812 zurückbrachte. Als ein Offizier von höherem Rang ritt er und trägt somit hohe Stiefel. Der Stock war ein Zeichen des Offiziersrang. **B3:** Der preussische Einfluss kann bei dieser Uniform gesehen werden. Die Hörner ersetzten die Trommeln in den Einheiten der leichten Infanterie; 'Schwalbennester' schmückten die Schultern der Musiker.

C1: Bemerke, das Haar nicht mehr zum Zopf gebunden und der Rock wird nun taillennah getragen. Die Quellennachweise unterscheiden sich in der Farbe der Federbusche – diese Zusammenstellung scheint wahrscheinlich zu sein. **C2:** Kavalleristen und Unteroffiziere dieser Eliteeinheit, vom Adel angezogen, hatten Offiziersrang im Verhältnis zu den Männern anderer Einheiten. **C3:** Französische Rangabzeichen wurden nun von allen Staatseinheiten getragen, doch die eigenartigen 'Contre-Epauletten' unterscheiden die Truppen von Hessen-Darmstadt.

D1: Der starke französische Einfluss ist an dieser Uniform klar zu erkennen. Nur wenige Soldaten waren an der Front in Spanien tatsächlich so ordentlich und vollkommen uniformiert wie hier abgebildet. **D2:** Der Ringkragen hat nun die Schärpe als Zeichen des Offiziersstandes ersetzt; und der Rock war über dem Bauch gerade geschnitten, die Weste verdeckend. **D3:** Das Regiment, total vernichtet bei der Berezina-Überquerung, trug nunmehr einen Helm nach bayrische Stilart anstelle des früheren englischen Stils.

E1: Kompanien dieser Elitefreiwilligen, die die traditionelle Jägeruniform und Gewehre trugen, waren den Conskribierten Infanteriebataillonen als Plänkler angeschlossen. **E2:** Blaue Hosen über den Stiefeln getragen ersetzten die weissen Kniebundhosen im Winter und während eines Feldzuges. **E3:** Im Jahre 1813–14 gegründet, benutzte diese Einheit viel französische Ausrüstung. Die 'Contre-Epauletten' wurden im Jahr 1814 durch mehr herkömmliche Schulterklappen ersetzt.

F1: Unteroffiziere trugen immer noch Hellebarden zur Parade. Die Einzelheiten der Fusiliersmütze waren von Regiment zu Regiment verschieden. **F2:** Typisch für die Husarenuniform dieser Periode, beinhalter diese Ausstattung die gelben, ursprünglich der der türkischen Offizieren nachgeahmten, Stiefel. **F3:** Die meisten Infanterieregimenter schienen Negertrommlerjungen angestellt zu haben, deren Röcke mit Litzen reichverziert waren nach Mustern verschieden je nach Regiment.

G1: Österreichische Uniformarten und Ausrüstung wurden von diesem kurzlebigen Freiwilligenkorps benutzt. **G2:** Obwohl die Kürassen von dieser Einheit schon einige Jahre vorher abgeschafft wurden, zeigt der Schnitt der Kollett immer noch die Ursprünge der Uniform. Trompeter unterschieden sich dadurch, dass sie glatt rasiert waren, durch ihre Ärmel-und Schulterauszeichnungen und durch Federbüschel mit roten Spitzen und rotem Unterteil. **G3:** Beachte den starken österreichischen Einfluss. Der Pelz an der Bärenfellmütze war so angebracht, dass er vorne nach oben und an den Seiten und hinten nach unten verlief. Beachte das fein eingravierte Bajonett, mit Hoheitsabzeichen.

H1: Der starke preussische Einfluss ist an dieser Uniform klar erkennbar. **H2:** Das gezopfte Haar wurde bis 1816 nicht wieder eingeführt. Typische Jägeruniform, einschliesslich Hirschfänger mit Hirschhorngriff. **H3:** Das russiche 'Kiwer' Schako wurde nicht allgemein getragen, einige Truppen trugen es nach preussischem Muster. Tresse-Knopflochschlingen an den Ärmelaufschlägen waren gelb oder gold je nach Rang.